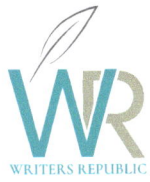

WRITERS REPUBLIC

I KNOW MY COLORS

Frelisha M. Jefferson

WRITERS REPUBLIC L.L.C.
515 Summit Ave. Unit R1
Union City, NJ 07087, USA

Website:	*www.writersrepublic.com*
Hotline :	*1-877-656-6838*
Email:	*info@writersrepublic.com*

Ordering Information:
Quantity sales. Special discounts are available on quantity purchases by corporations, associations, and others. For details, contact the publisher at the address above.

Library of Congress Control Number:	2022943945	
ISBN-13:	979-8-88536-520-8	[Paperback Edition]
	979-8-88536-615-1	[Hardback Edition]
	979-8-88536-521-5	[Digital Edition]

Rev. date: 07/28/2022

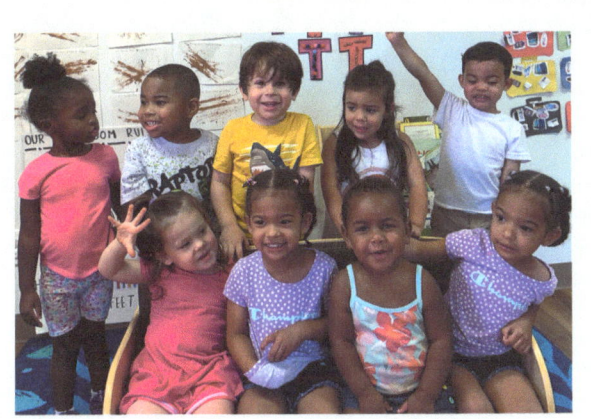

THiS BOOK iS DEDiCATED TO

my 2-year-olds, their interest in learning
has inspired me to write a learning book.
Love you all dearly and equally.

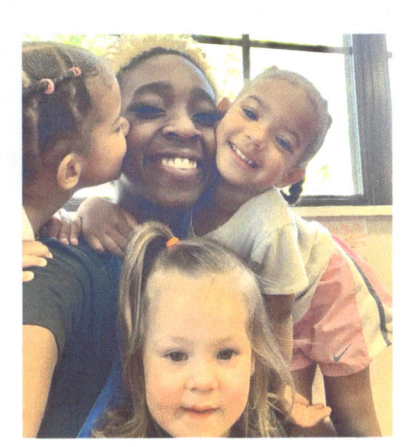

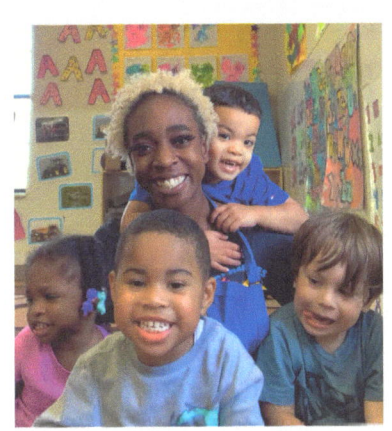

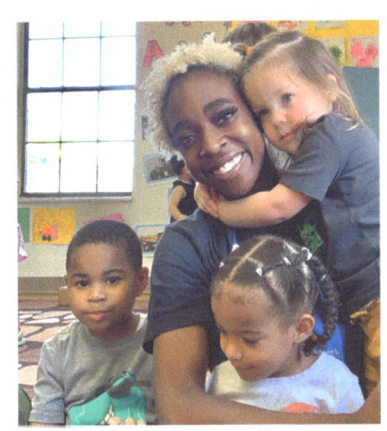

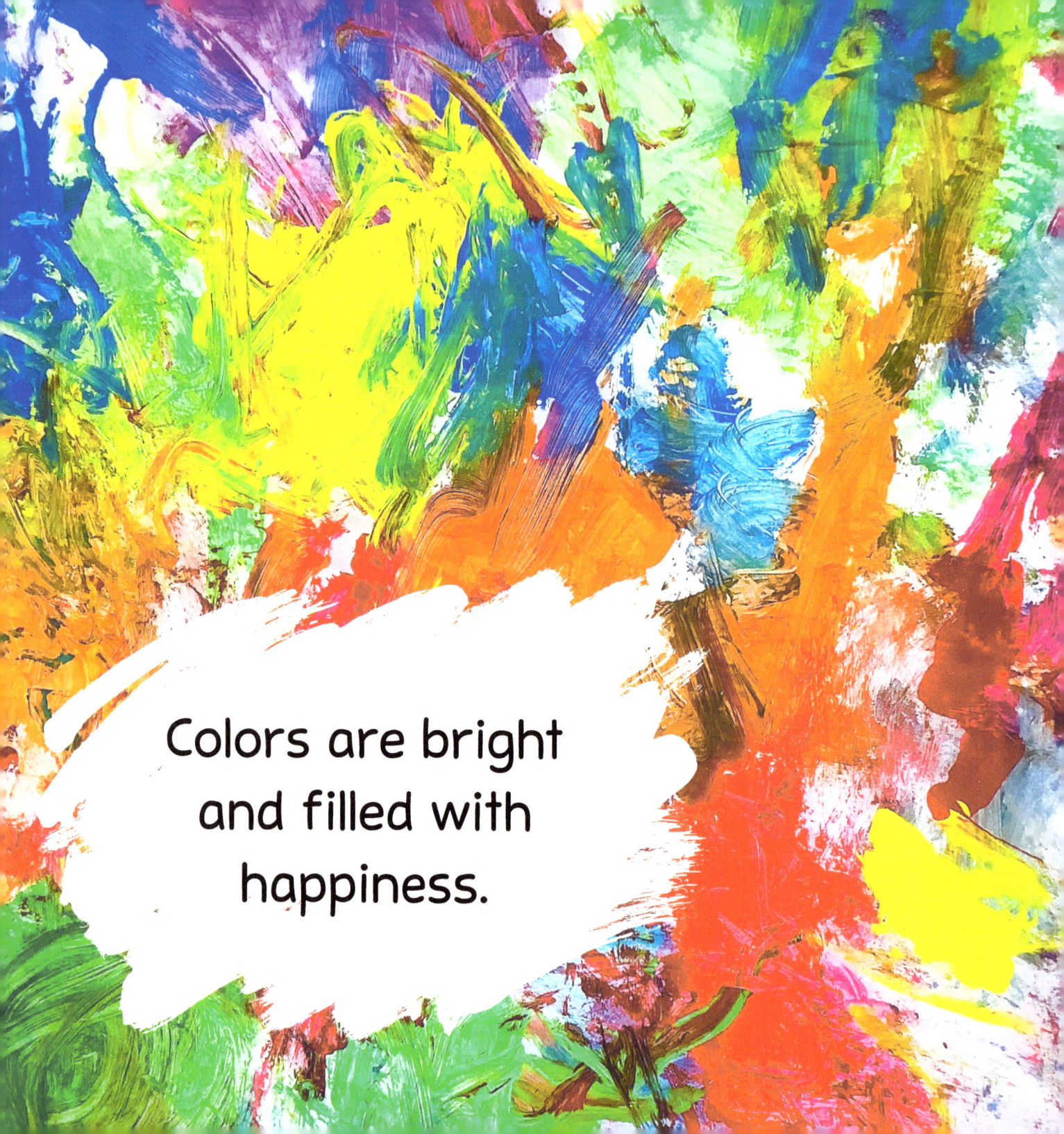

Colors are bright
and filled with
happiness.

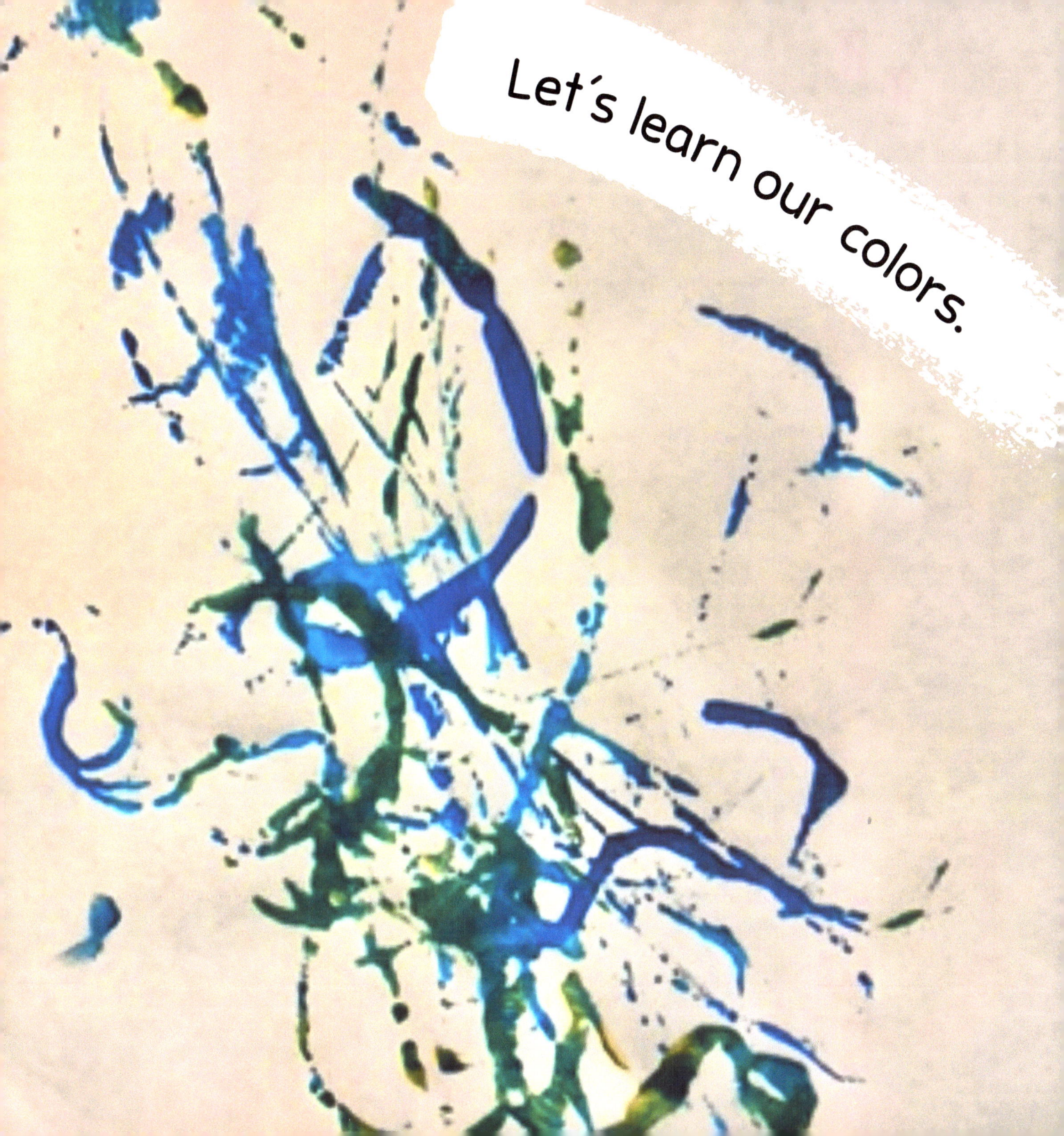

Let's learn our colors.

We see colors everyday
rather it's an object,
something we eat
or an animal.

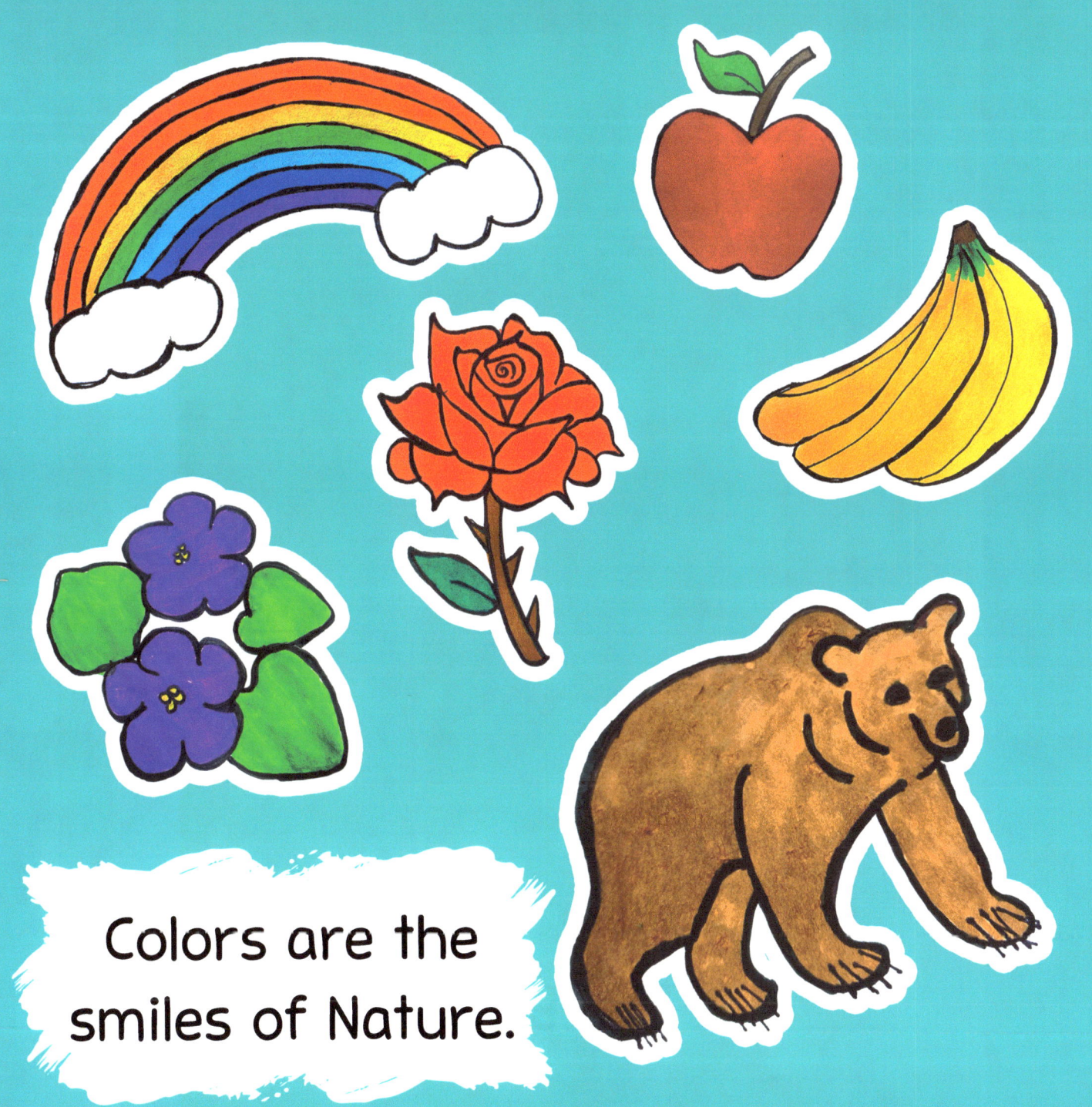

Colors are the smiles of Nature.

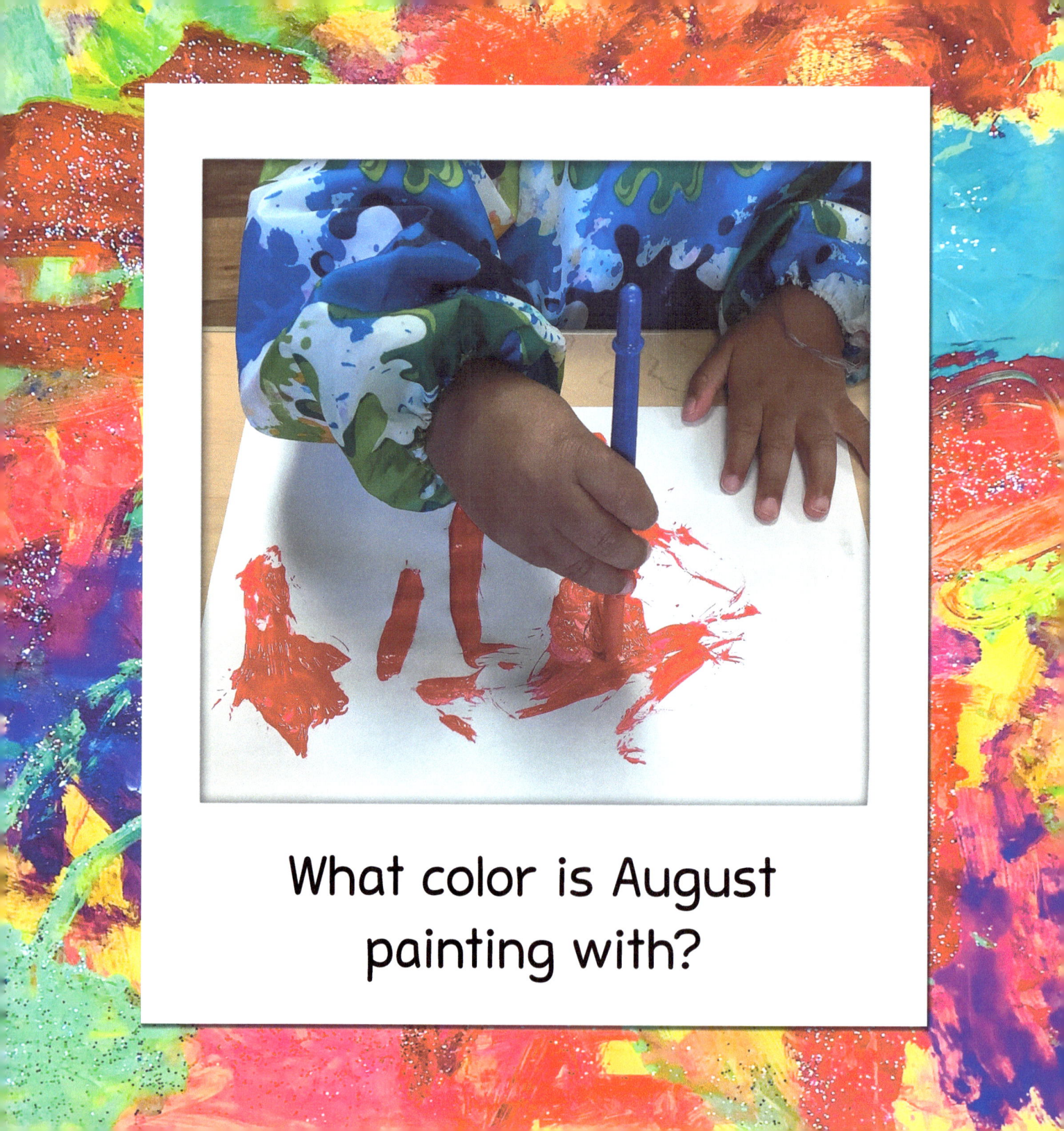

What color is August painting with?

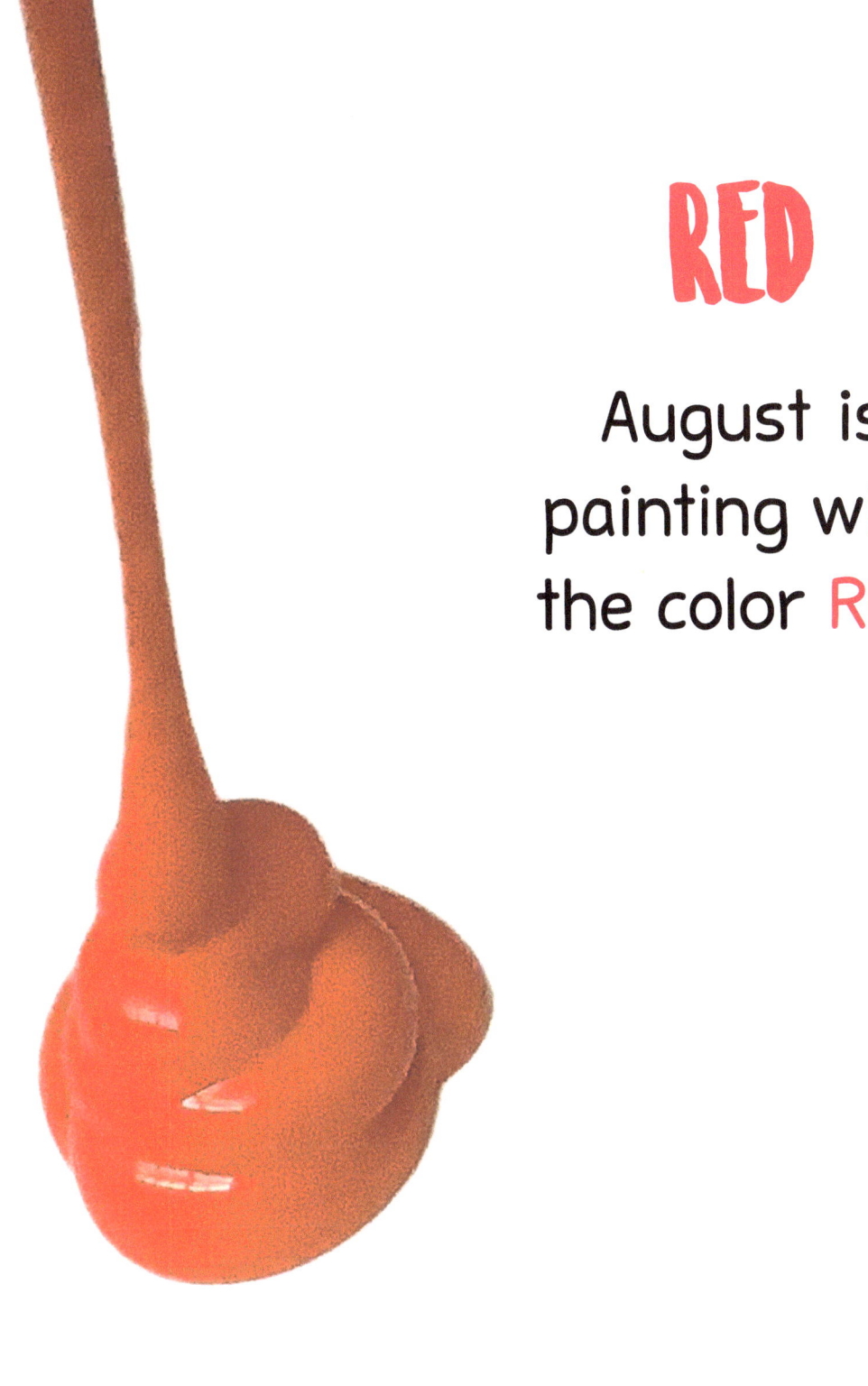

RED

August is
painting with
the color RED.

What is something that you know that's RED in color?

RED

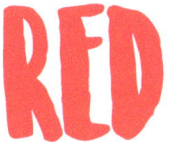

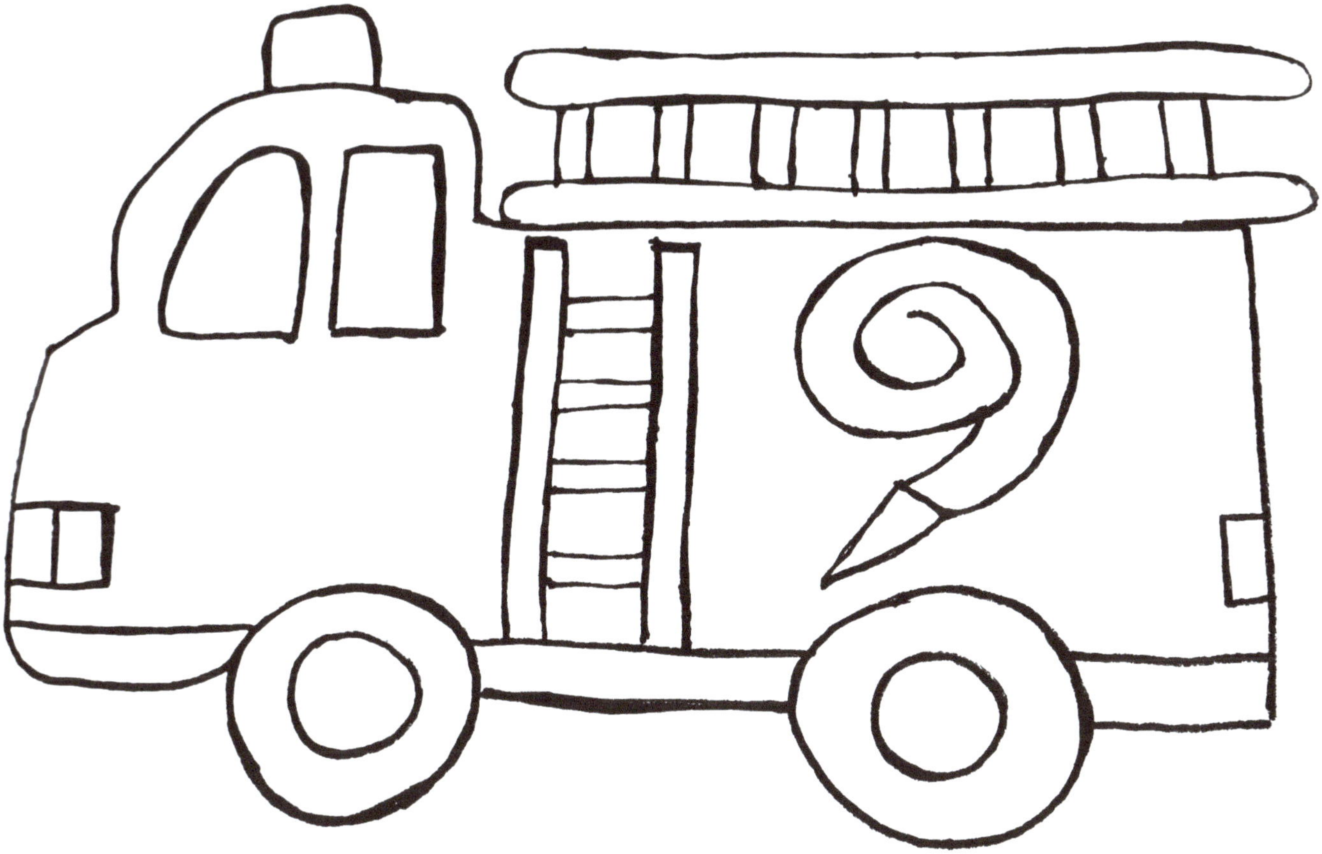

Color the FIRE TRUCK the color RED.

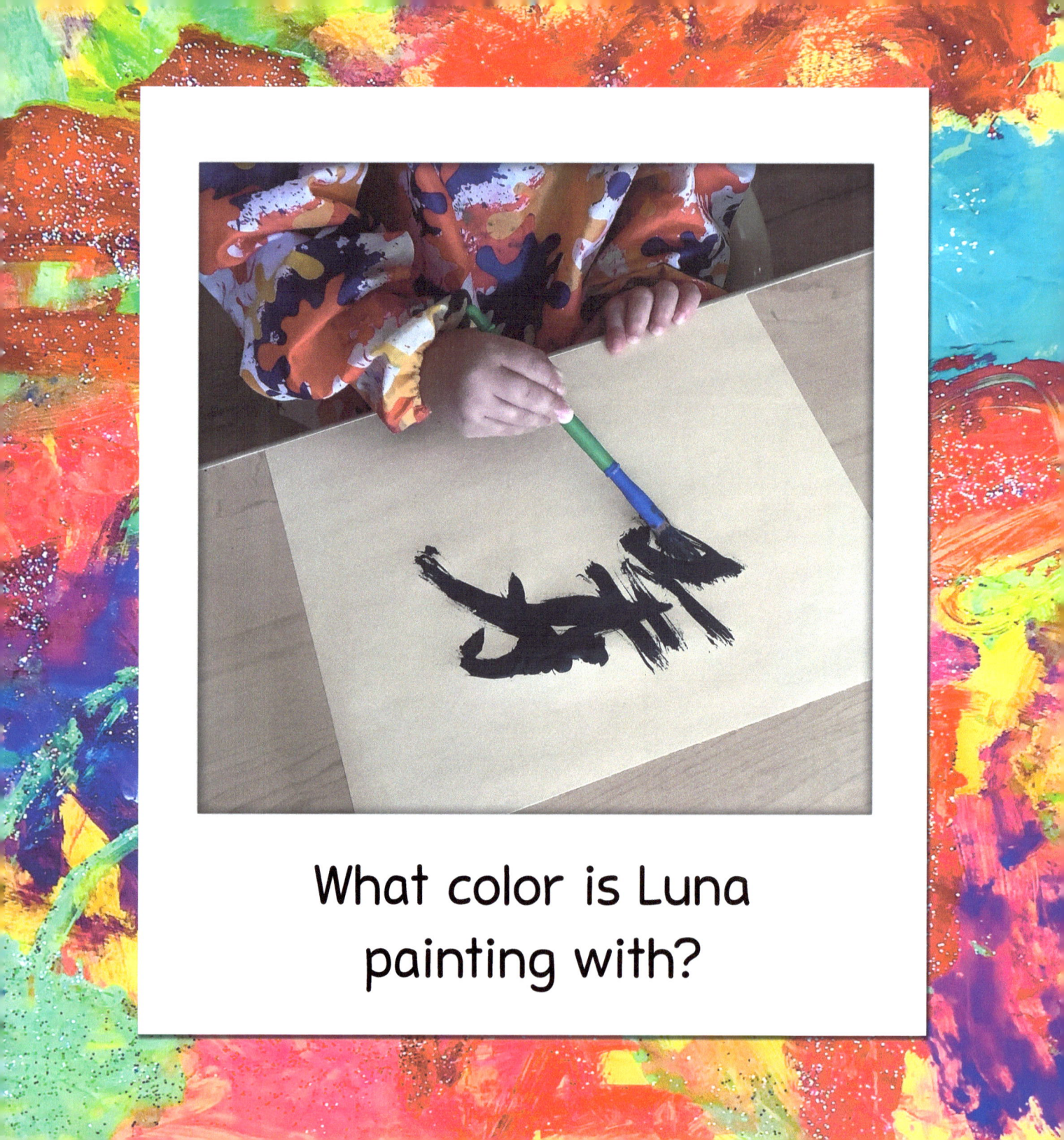

What color is Luna painting with?

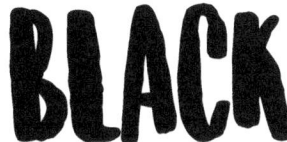

BLACK

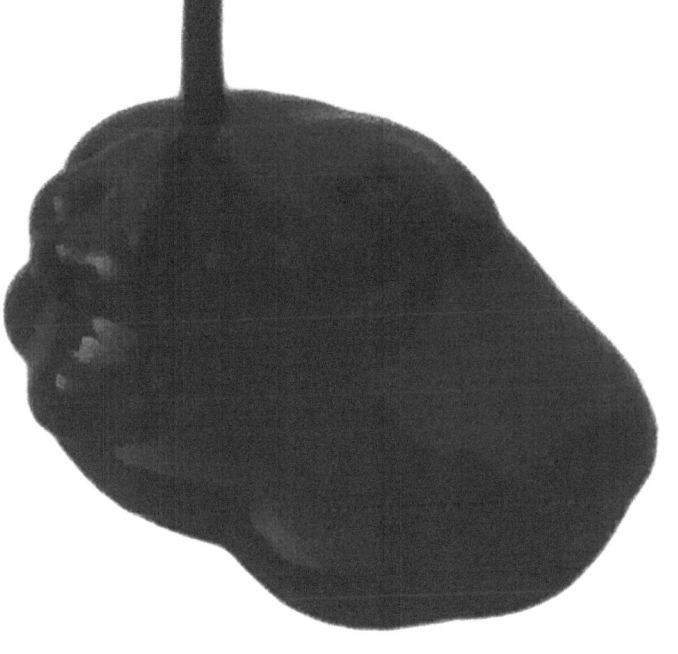

Luna is painting
with the color
BLACK.

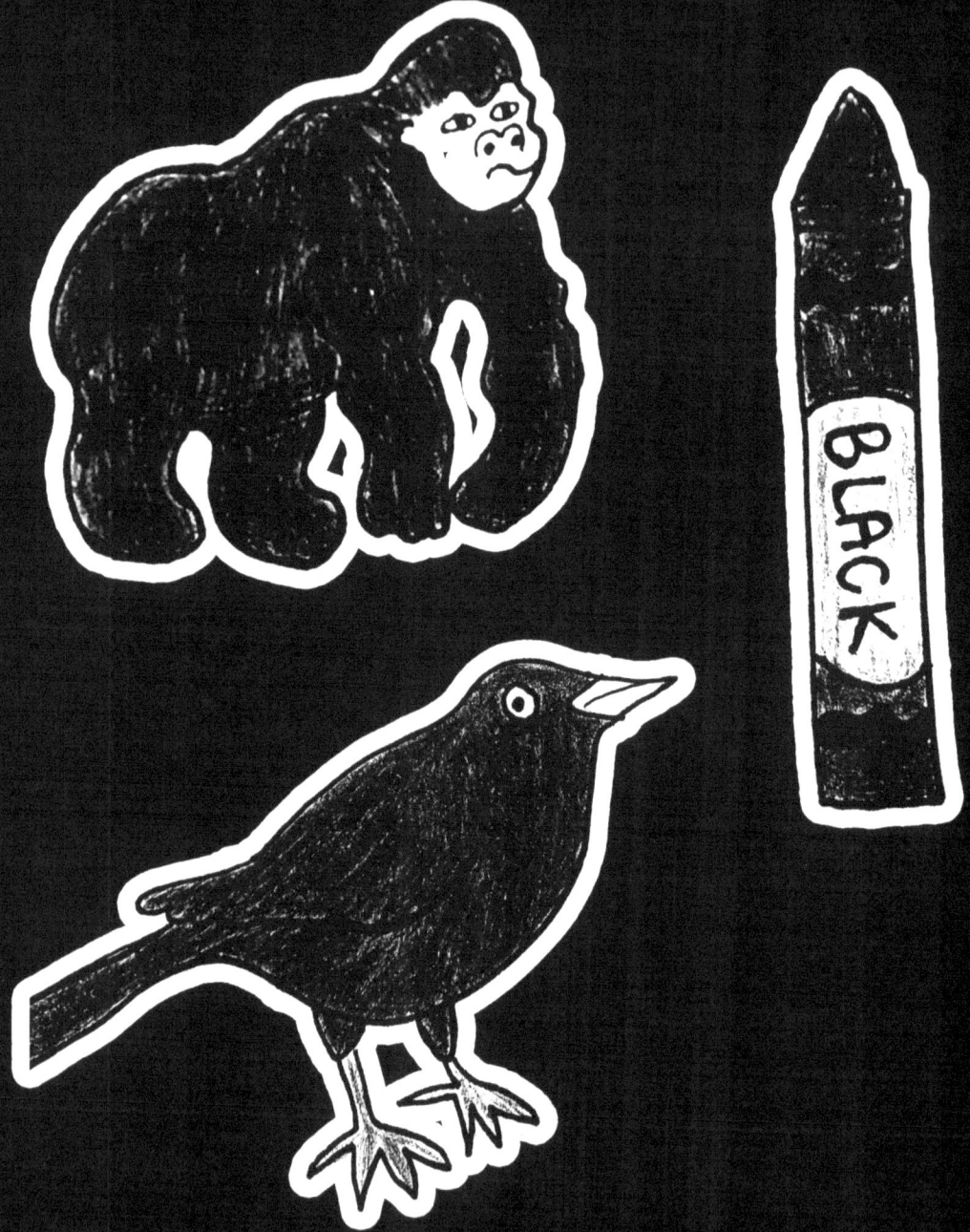

What is something that you know that's BLACK in color?

BLACK

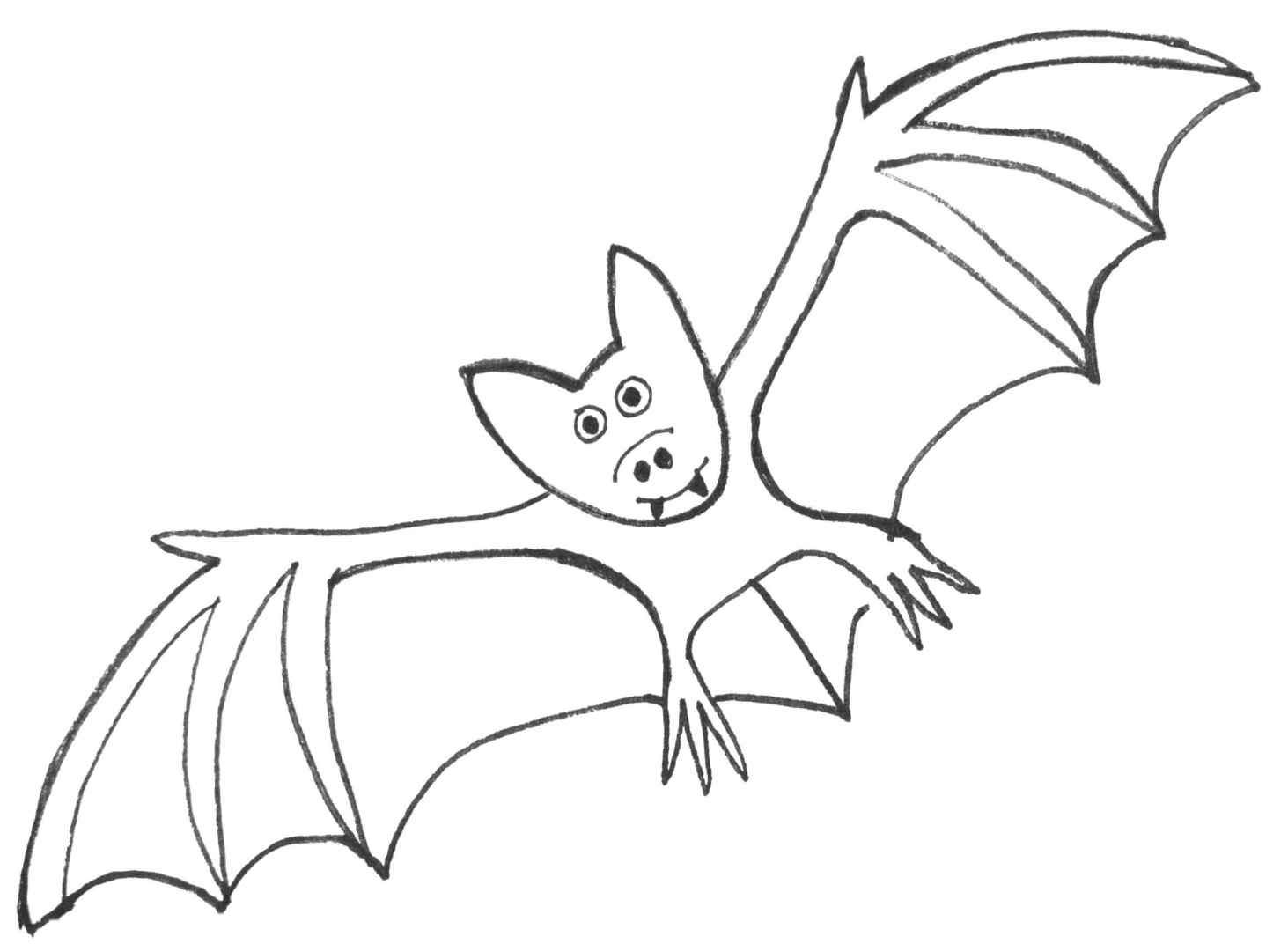

Color the BAT the color BLACK.

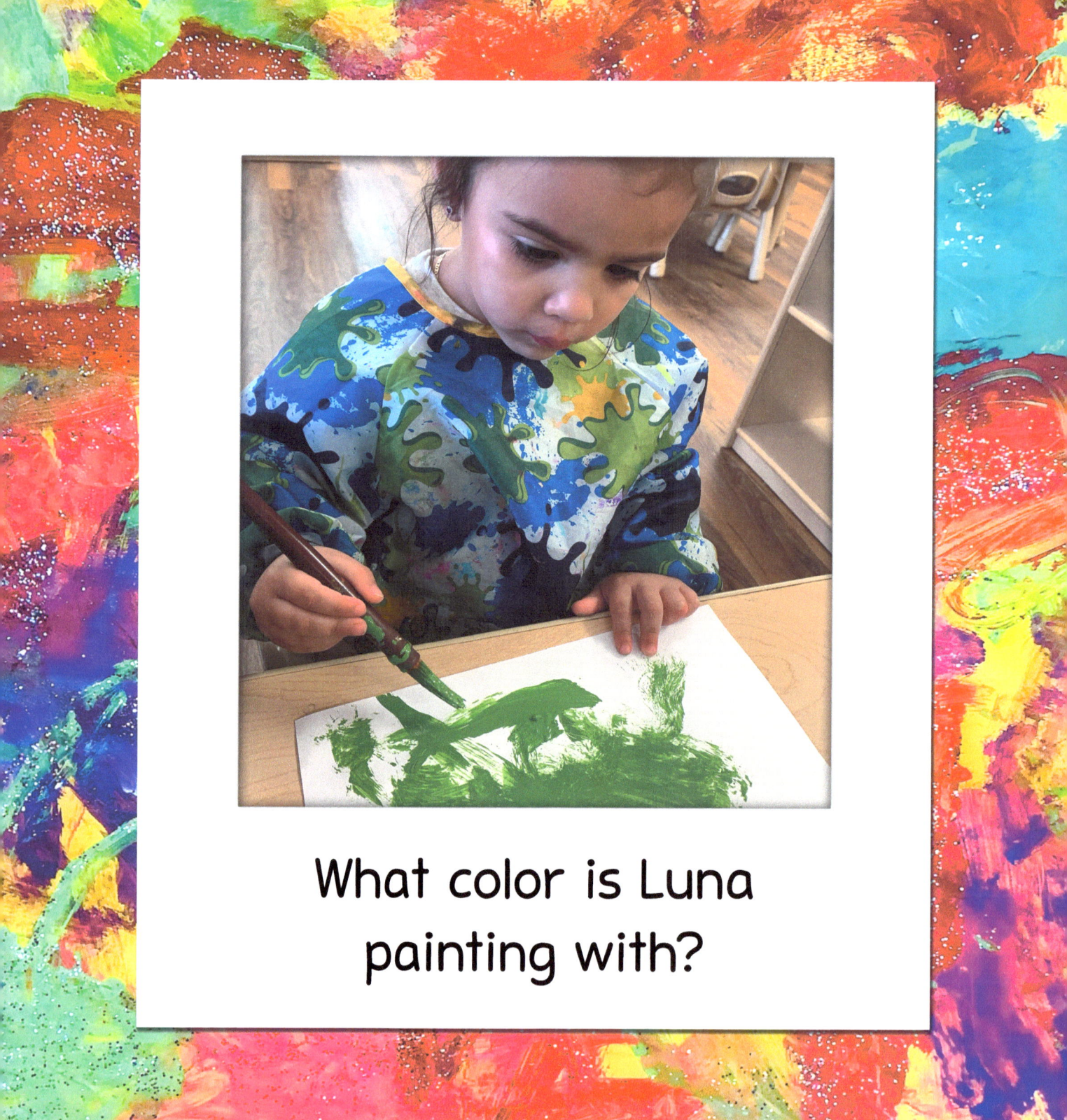

What color is Luna painting with?

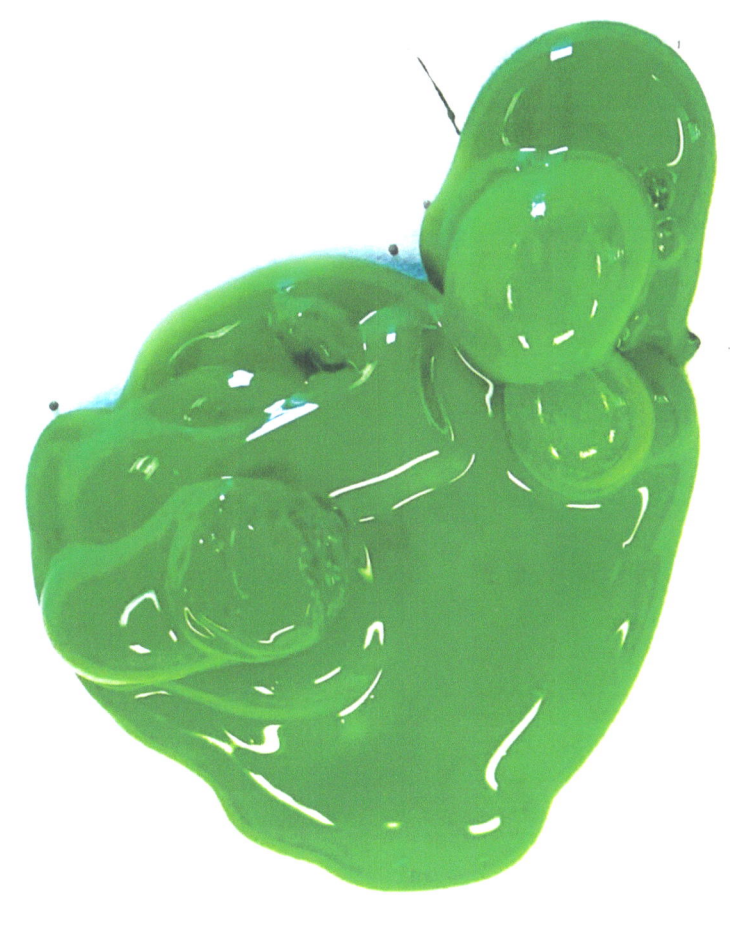

GREEN

Luna is painting
with the color
GREEN.

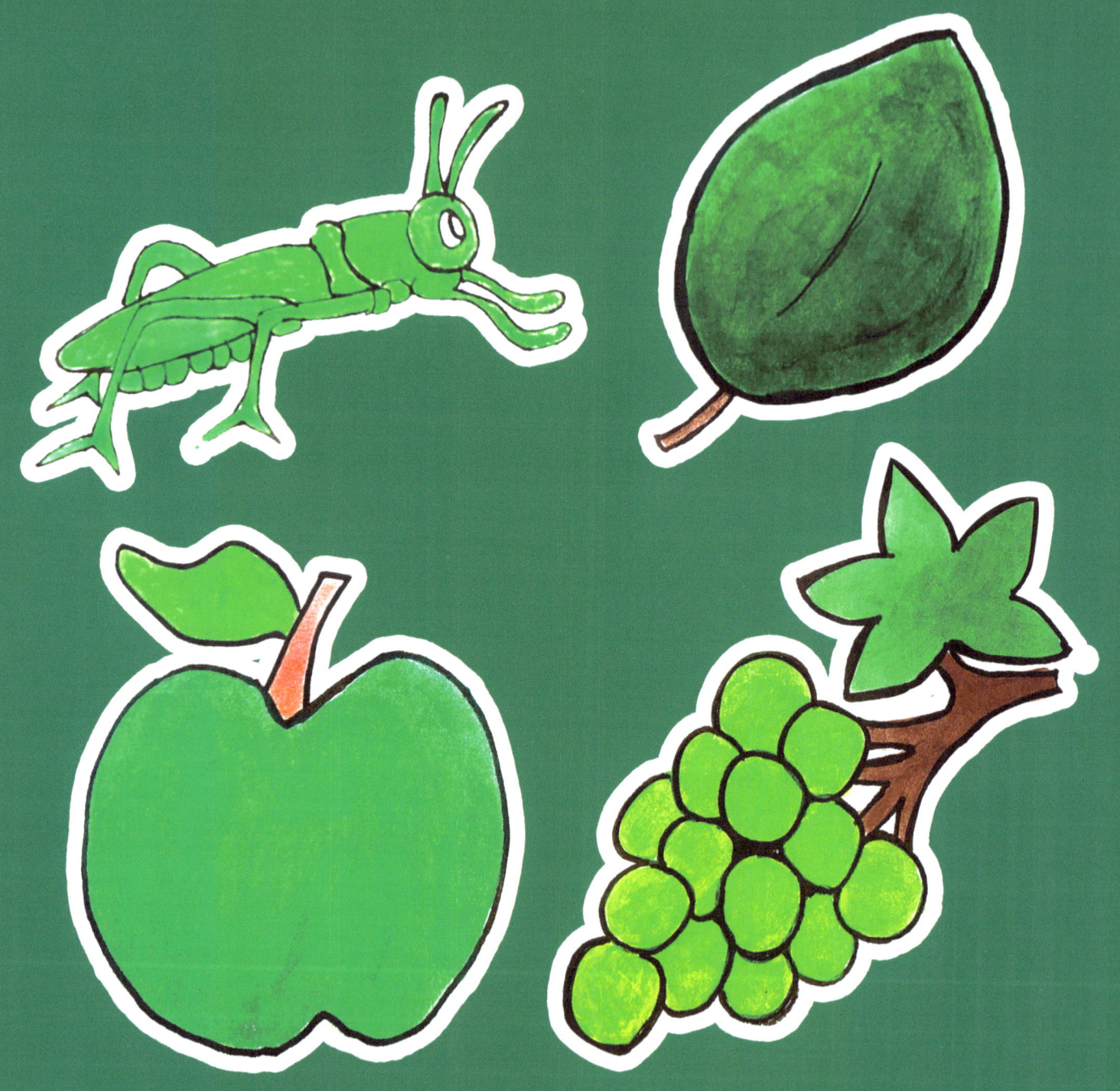

What is something that you know that's GREEN in color?

GREEN

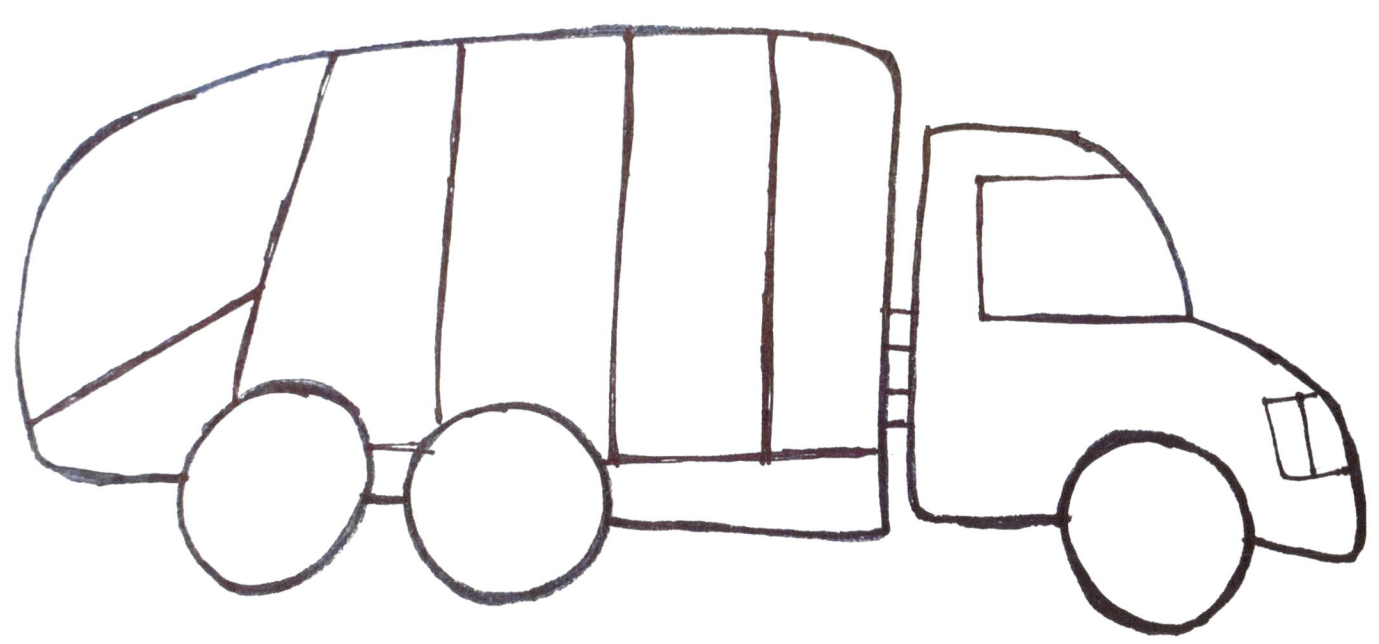

Color the GARBAGE TRUCK the color GREEN.

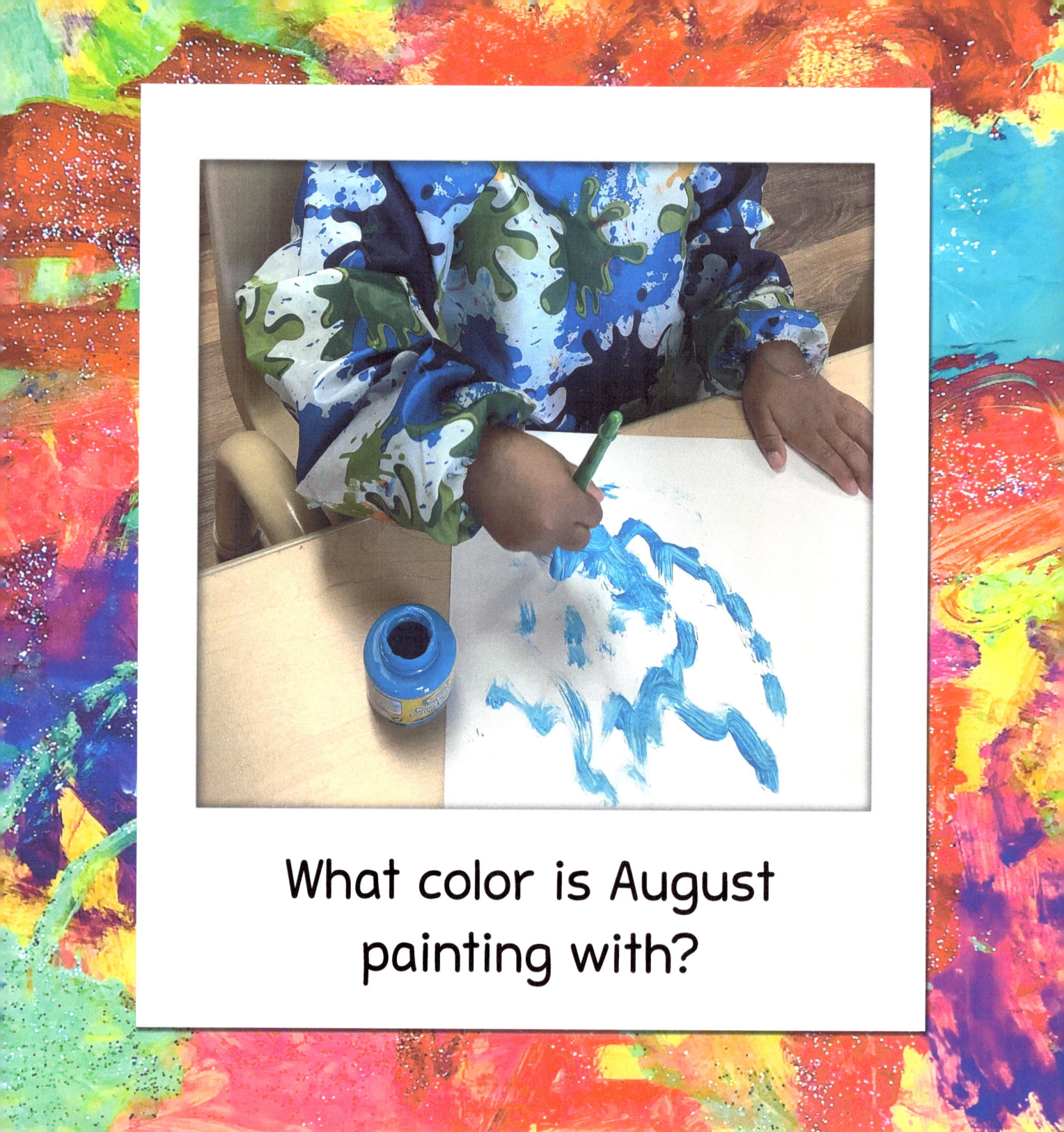

What color is August painting with?

BLUE

August is
painting with
the color BLUE.

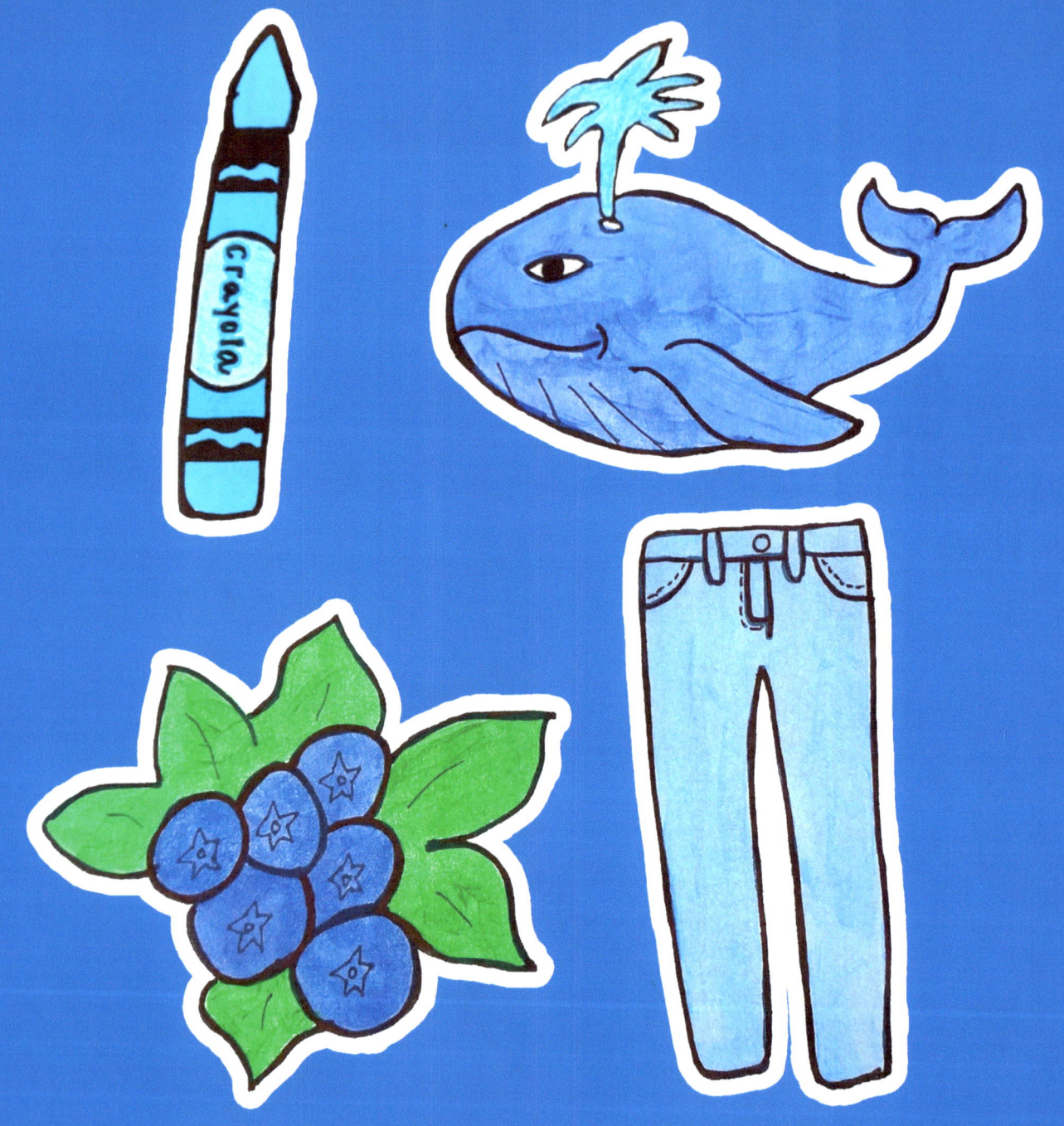

What is something that you know that's BLUE in color?

BLUE

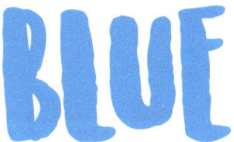

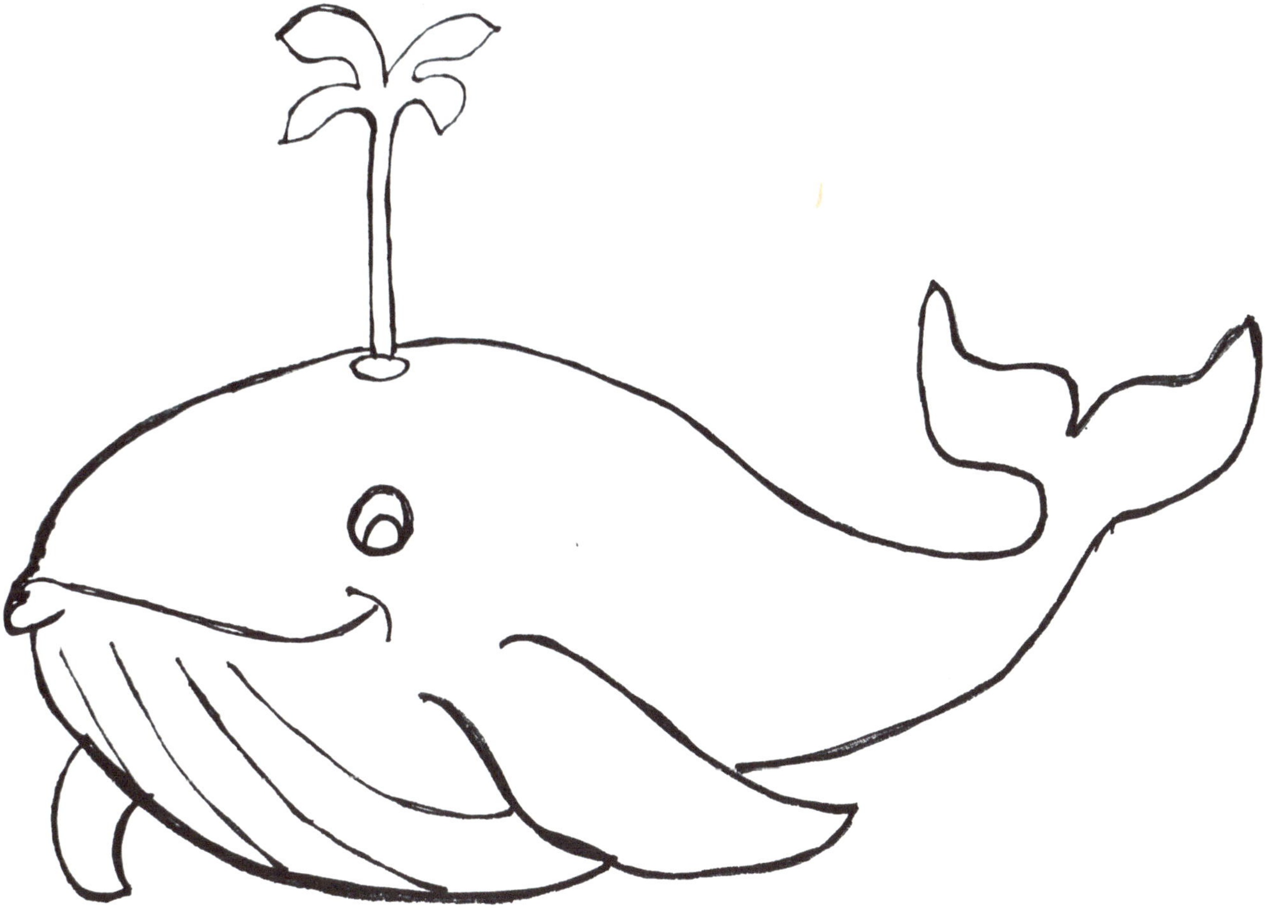

Color the WHALE the color BLUE.

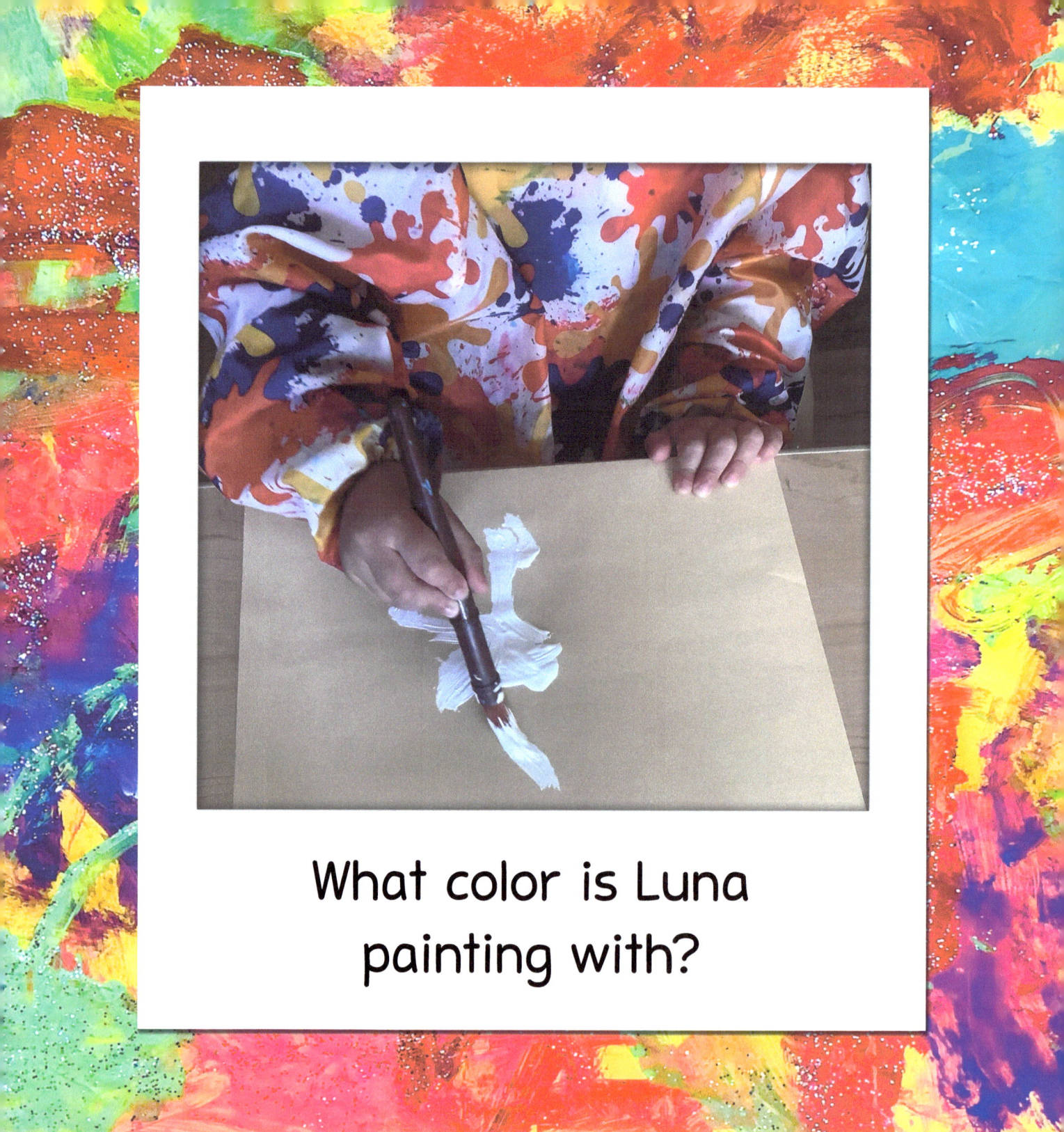

What color is Luna
painting with?

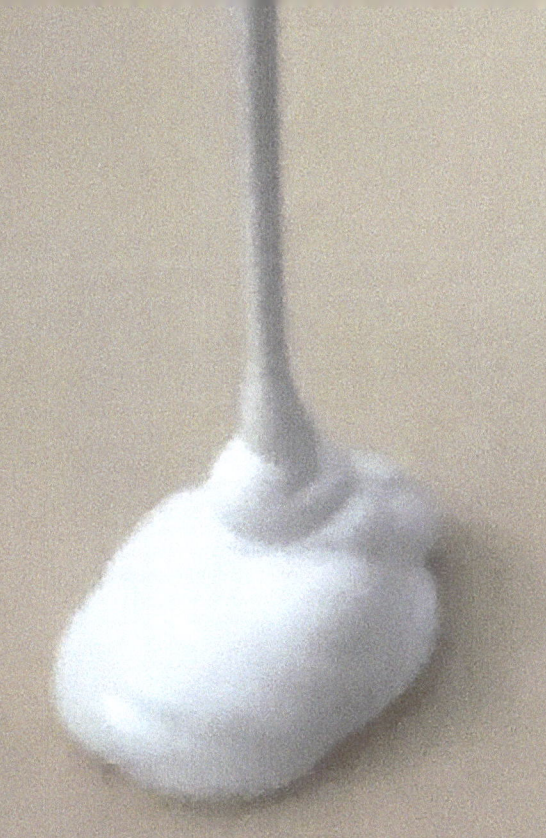

WHITE

Luna is painting with
the color WHITE.

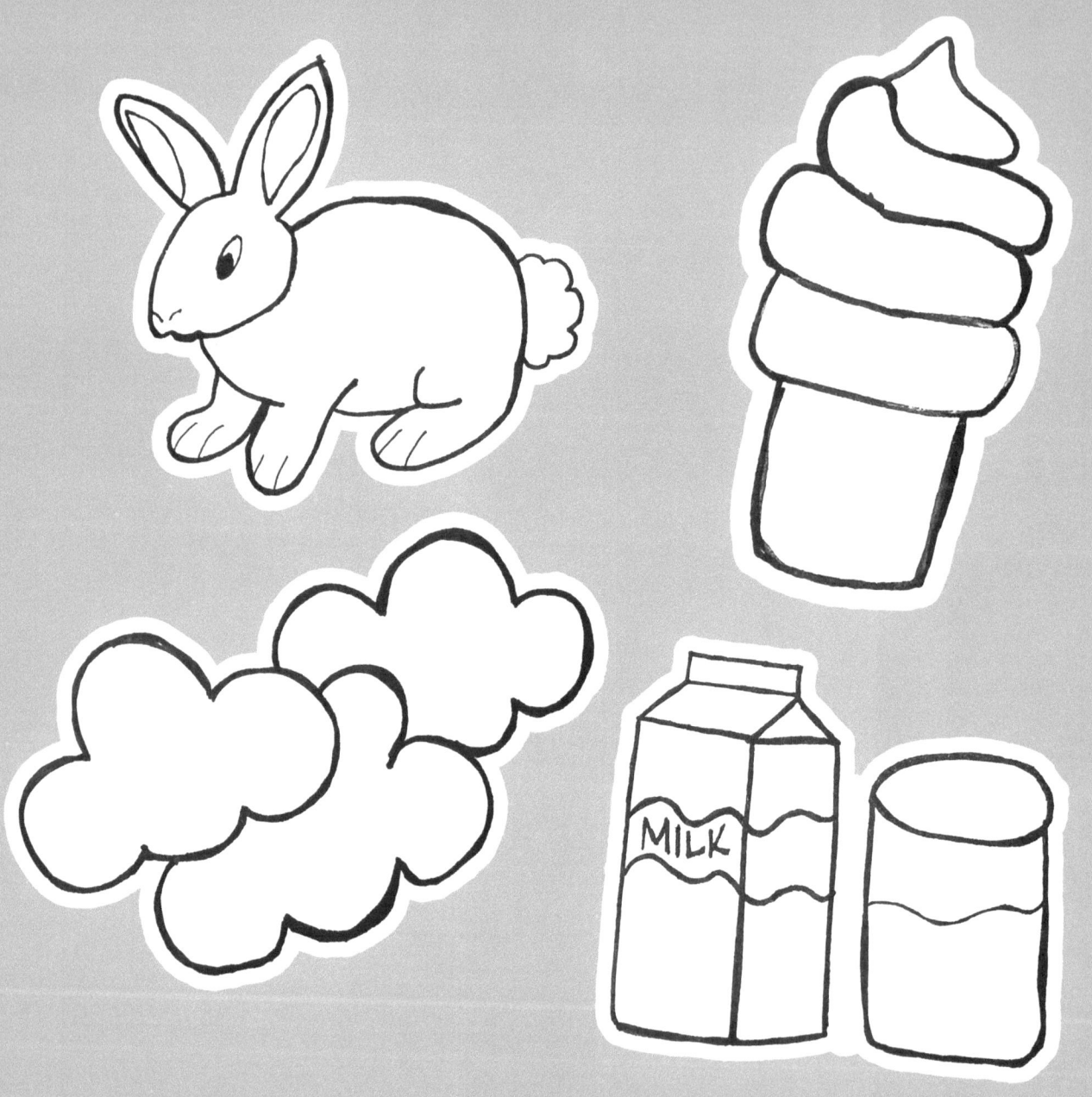

What is something that you know that's WHITE in color?

WHITE

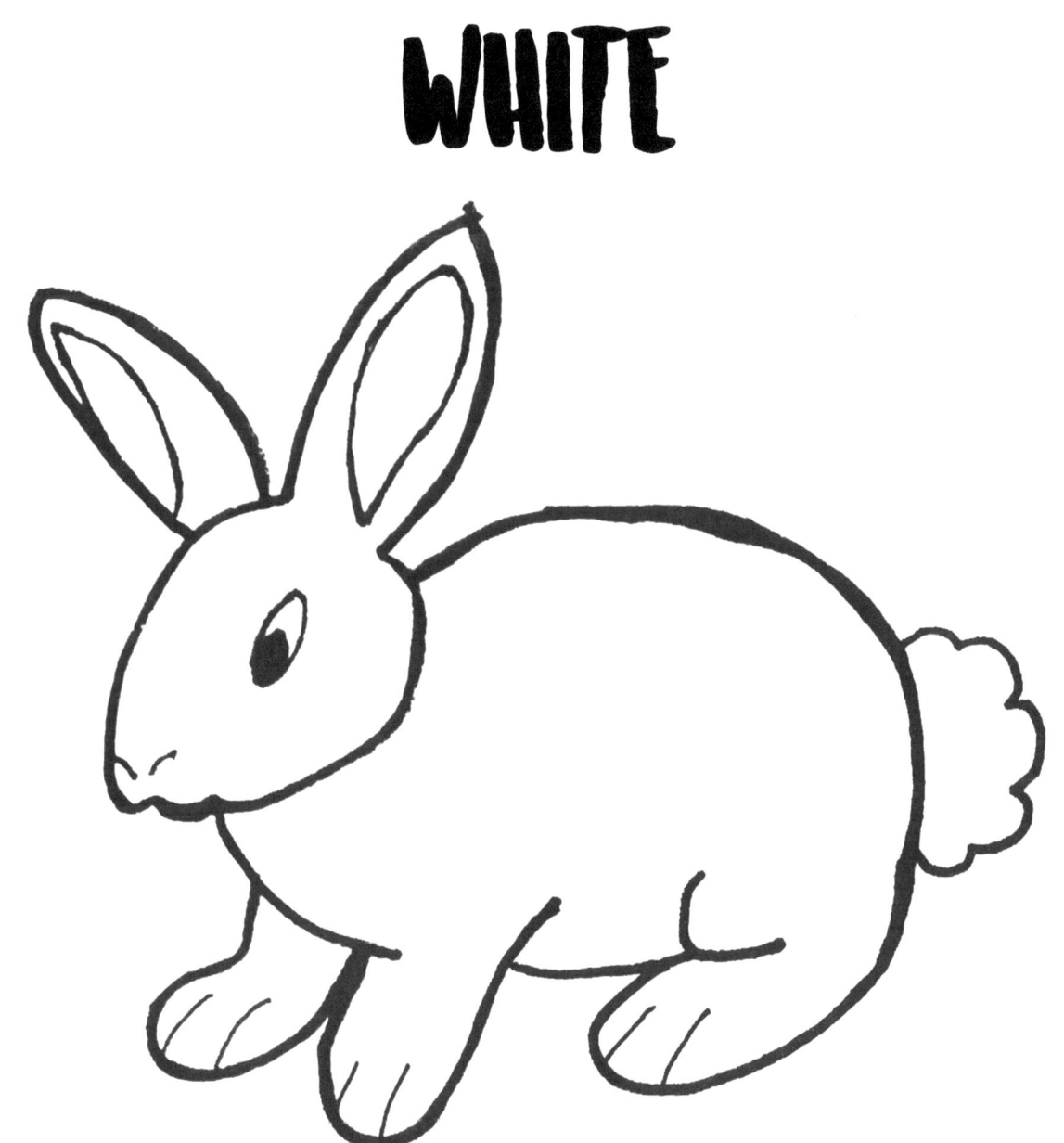

Color the RABBIT the color WHITE.

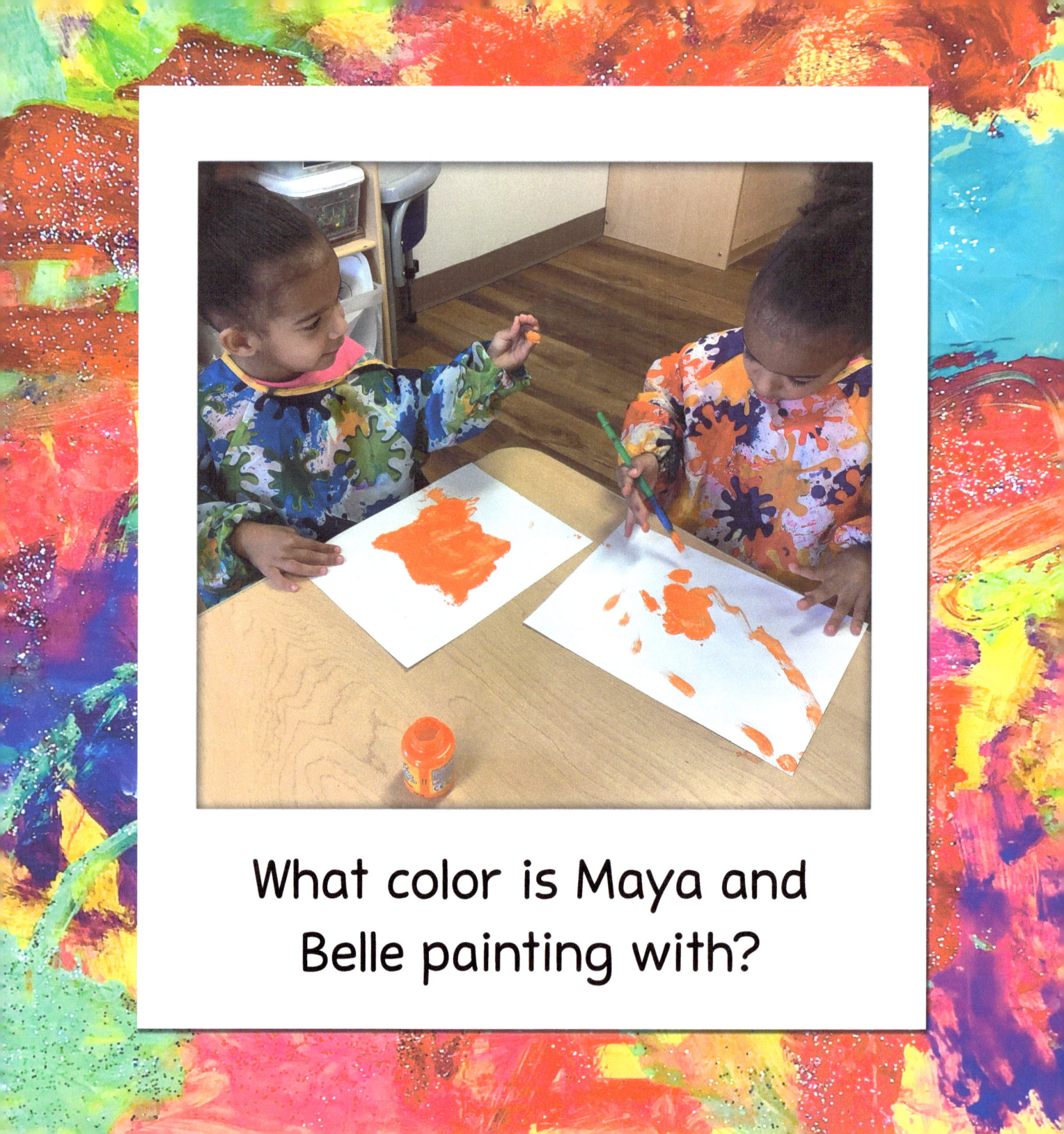

What color is Maya and Belle painting with?

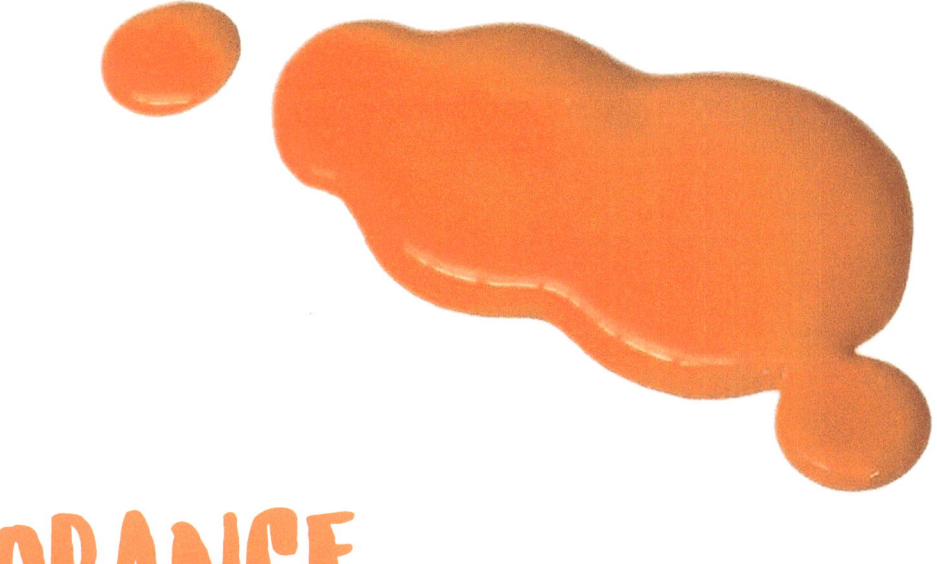

ORANGE

Maya and Belle are painting with the color ORANGE.

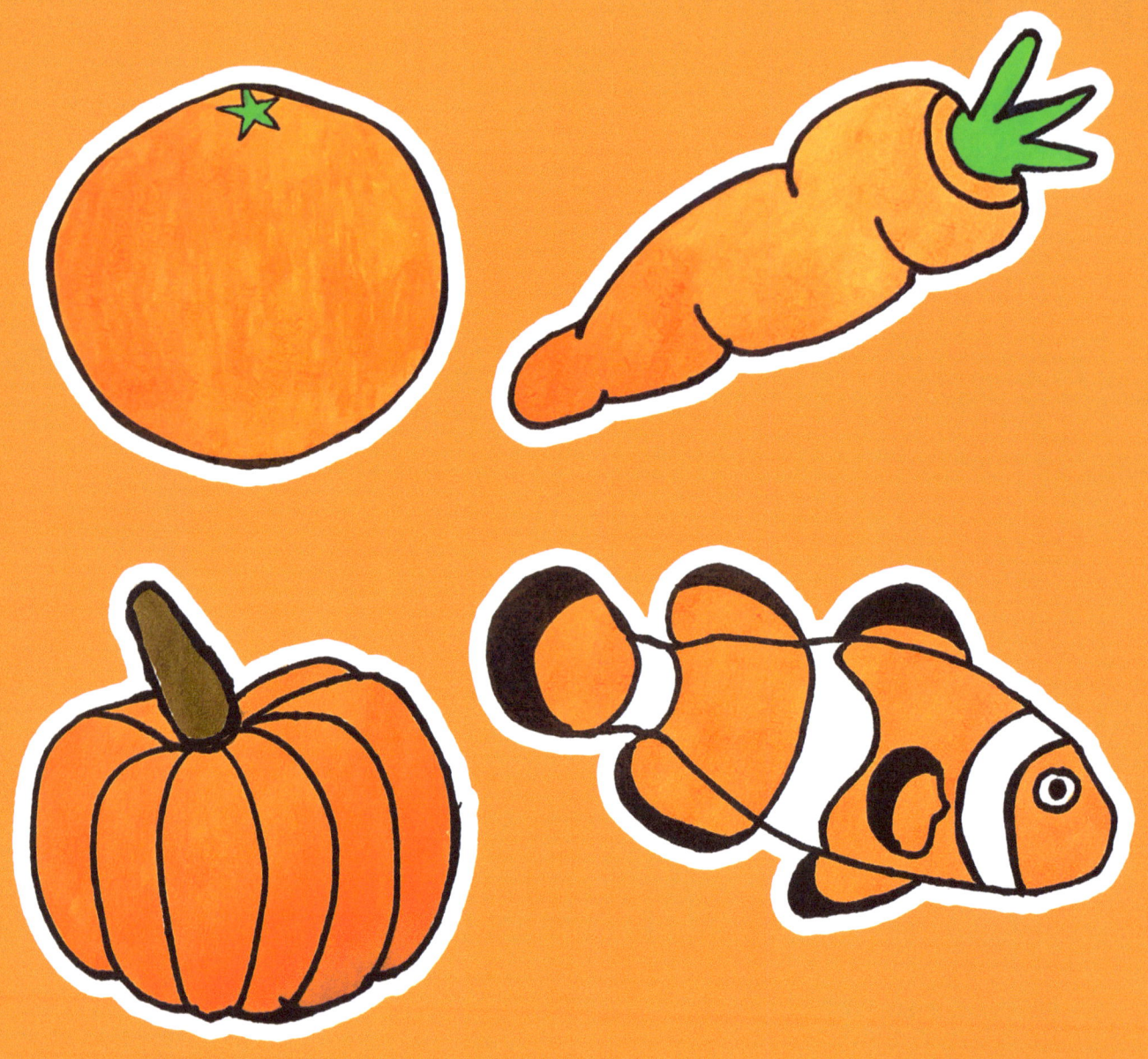

What is something that you know that's ORANGE in color?

ORANGE

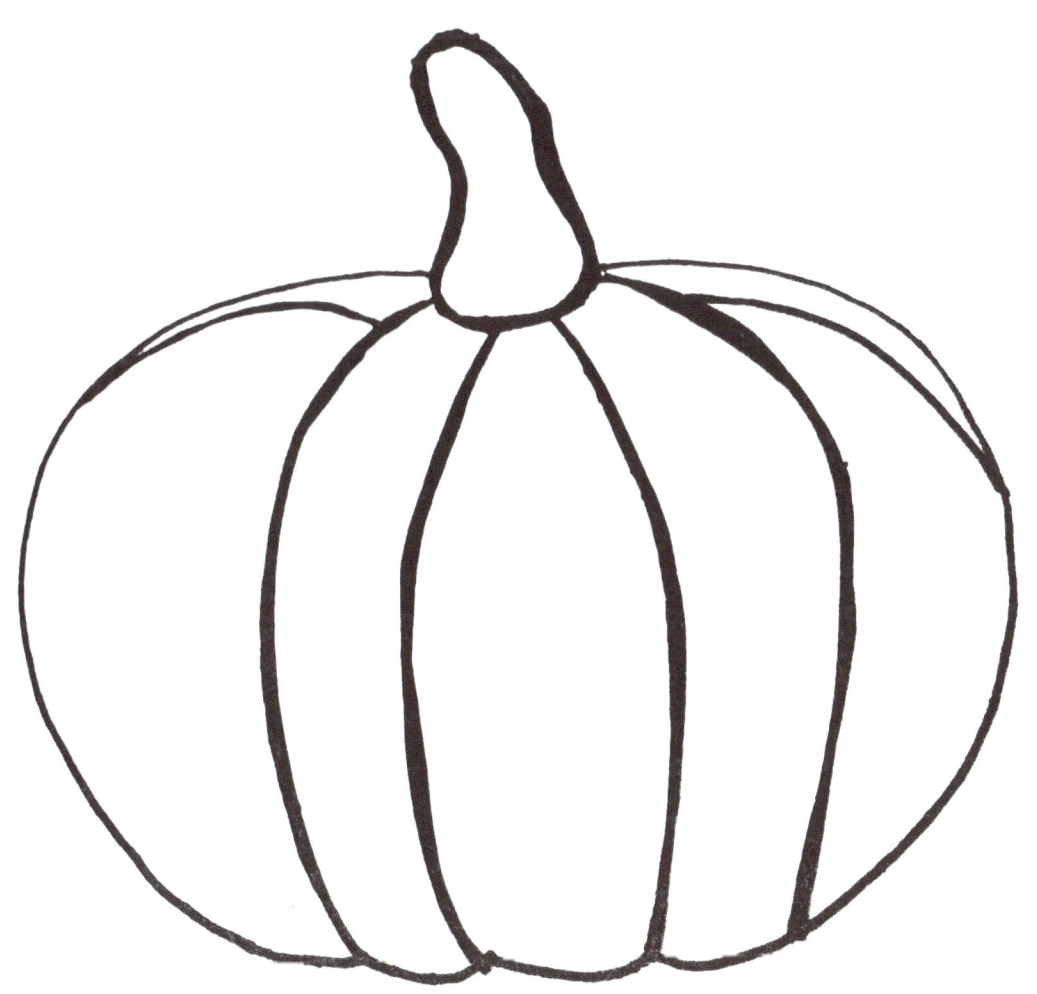

Color the PUMPKIN the color ORANGE.

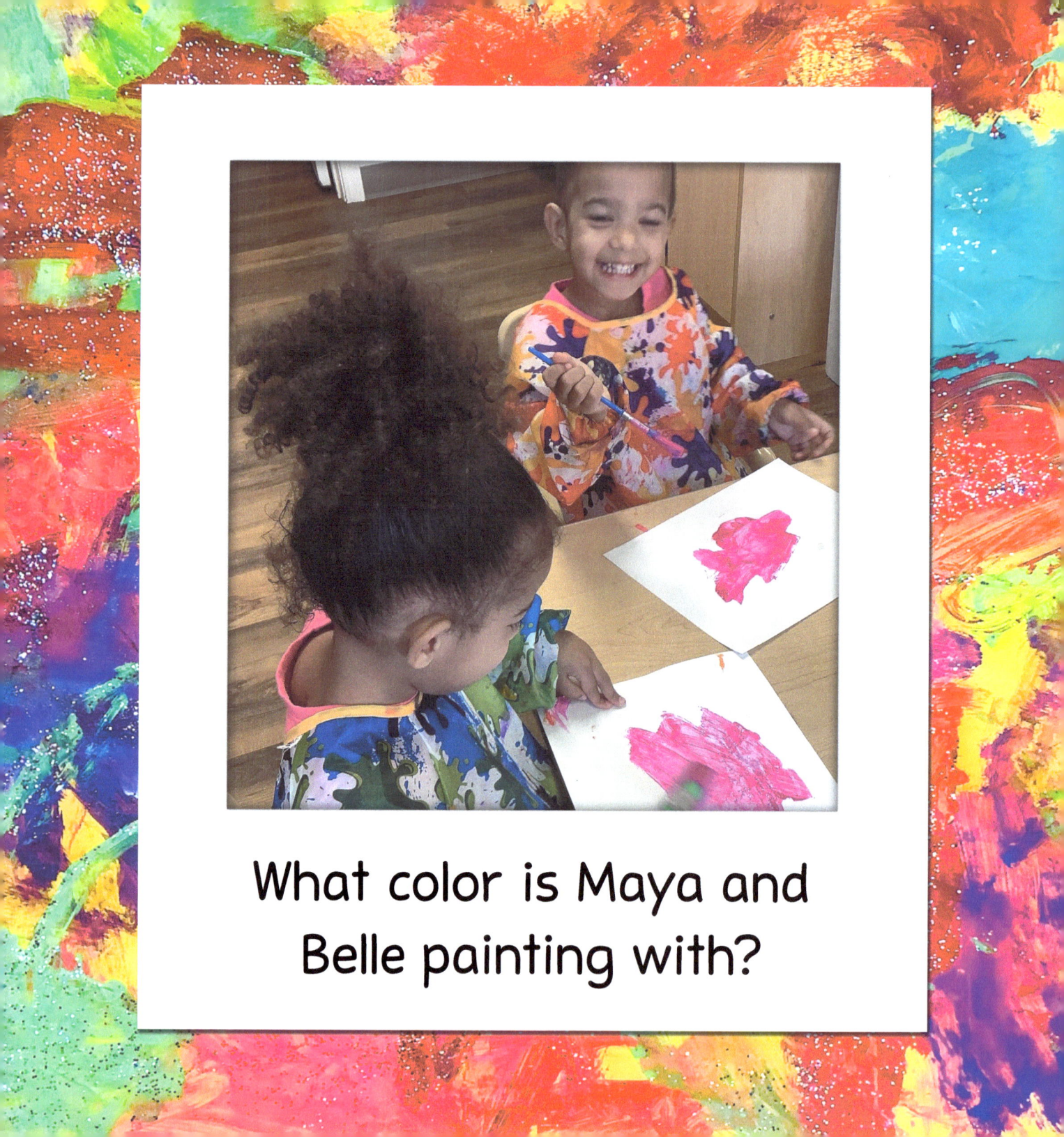

What color is Maya and
Belle painting with?

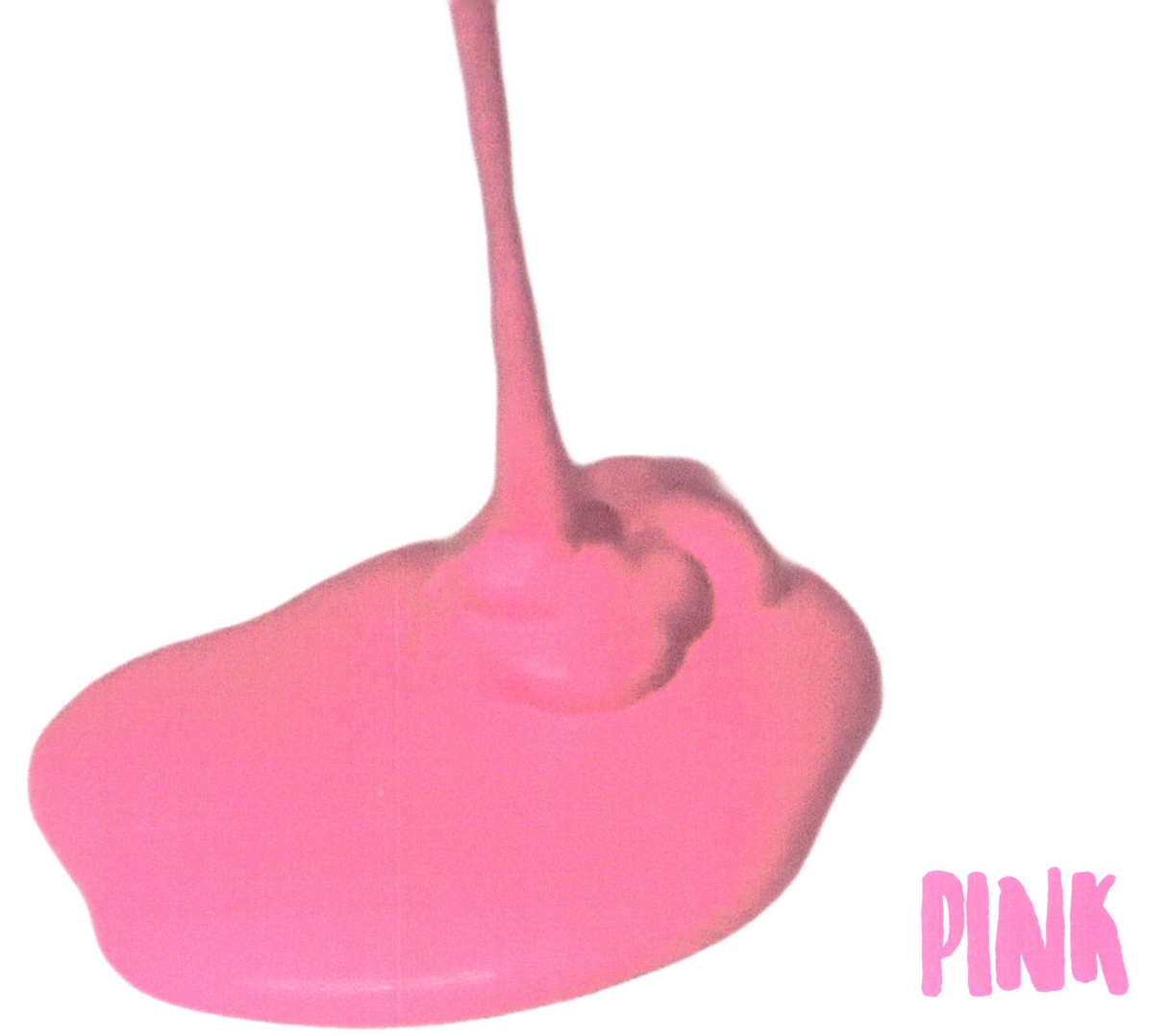

PINK

Maya & Belle are painting with the color PINK.

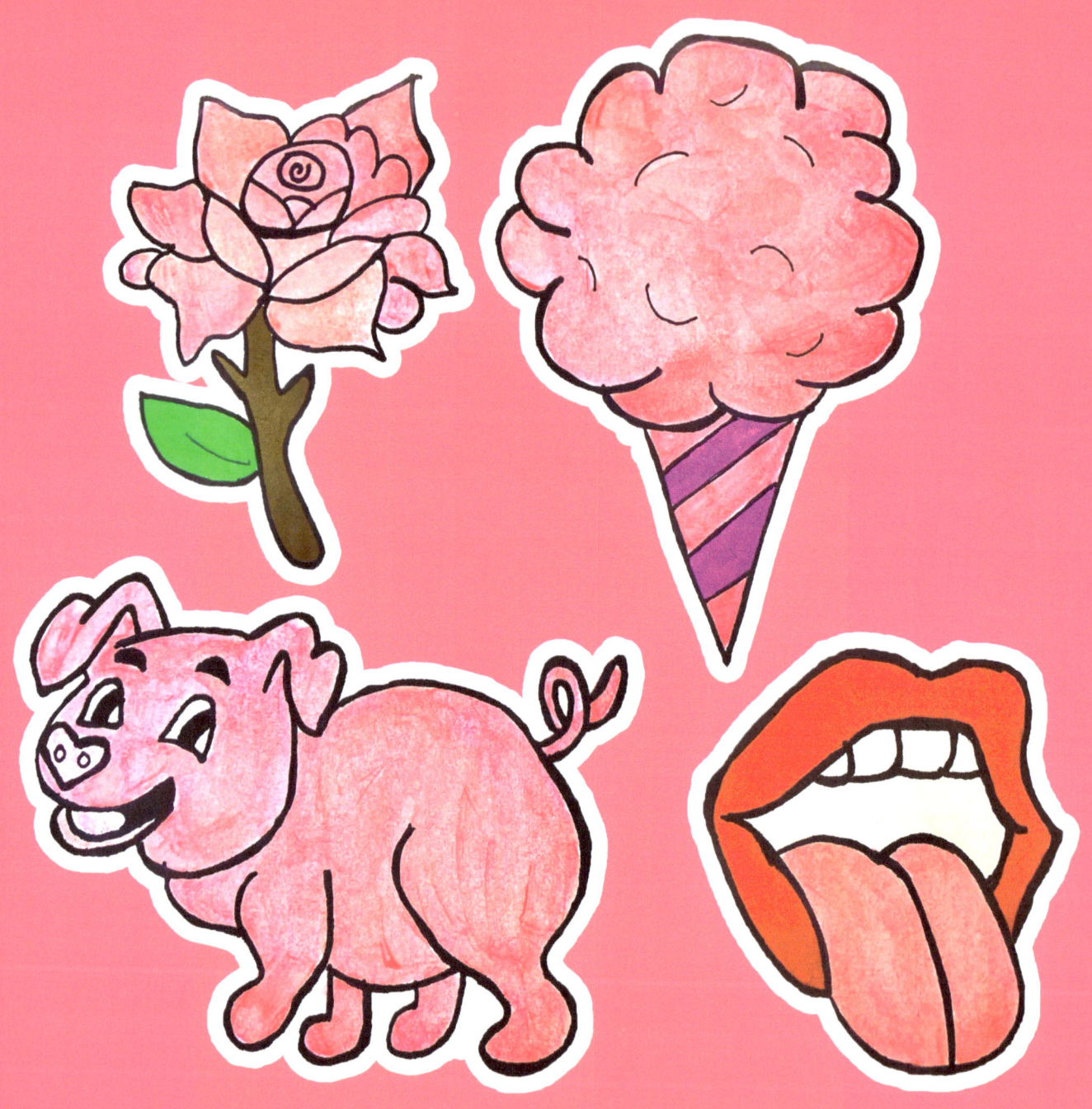

What is something that you know that's PINK in color?

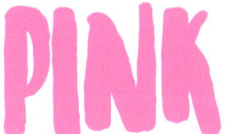

PINK

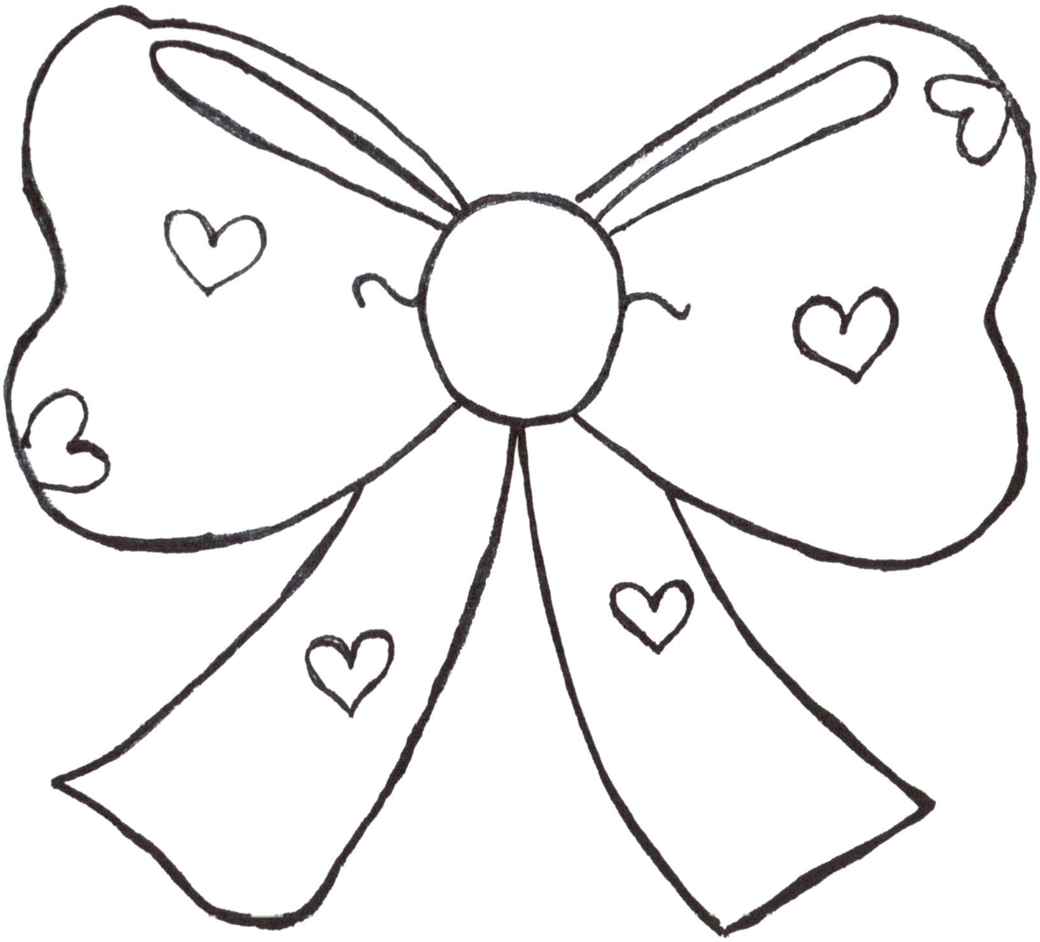

Color the RIBBON the color PINK.

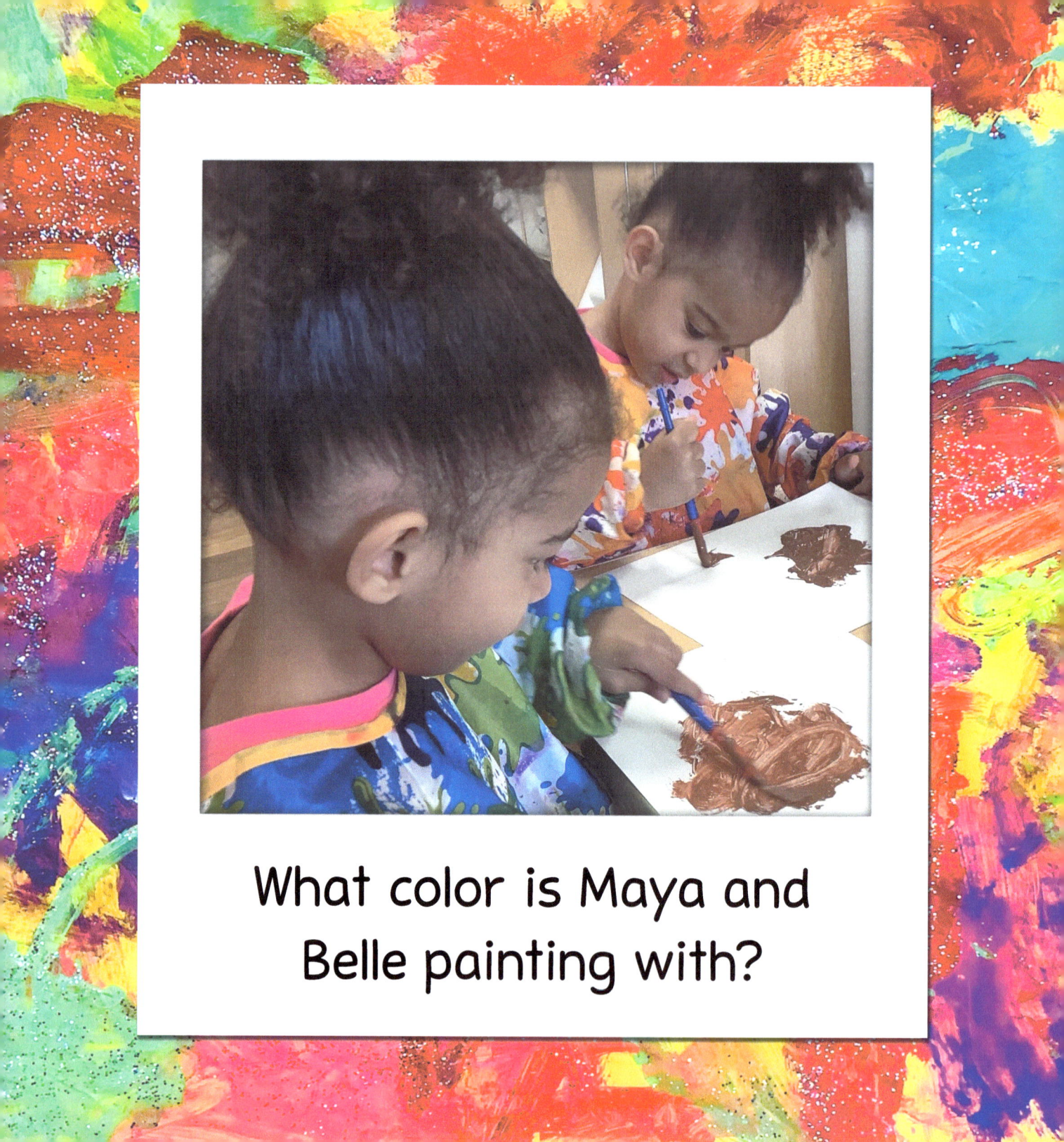

What color is Maya and Belle painting with?

BROWN

Maya and Belle
are painting
with the color
BROWN.

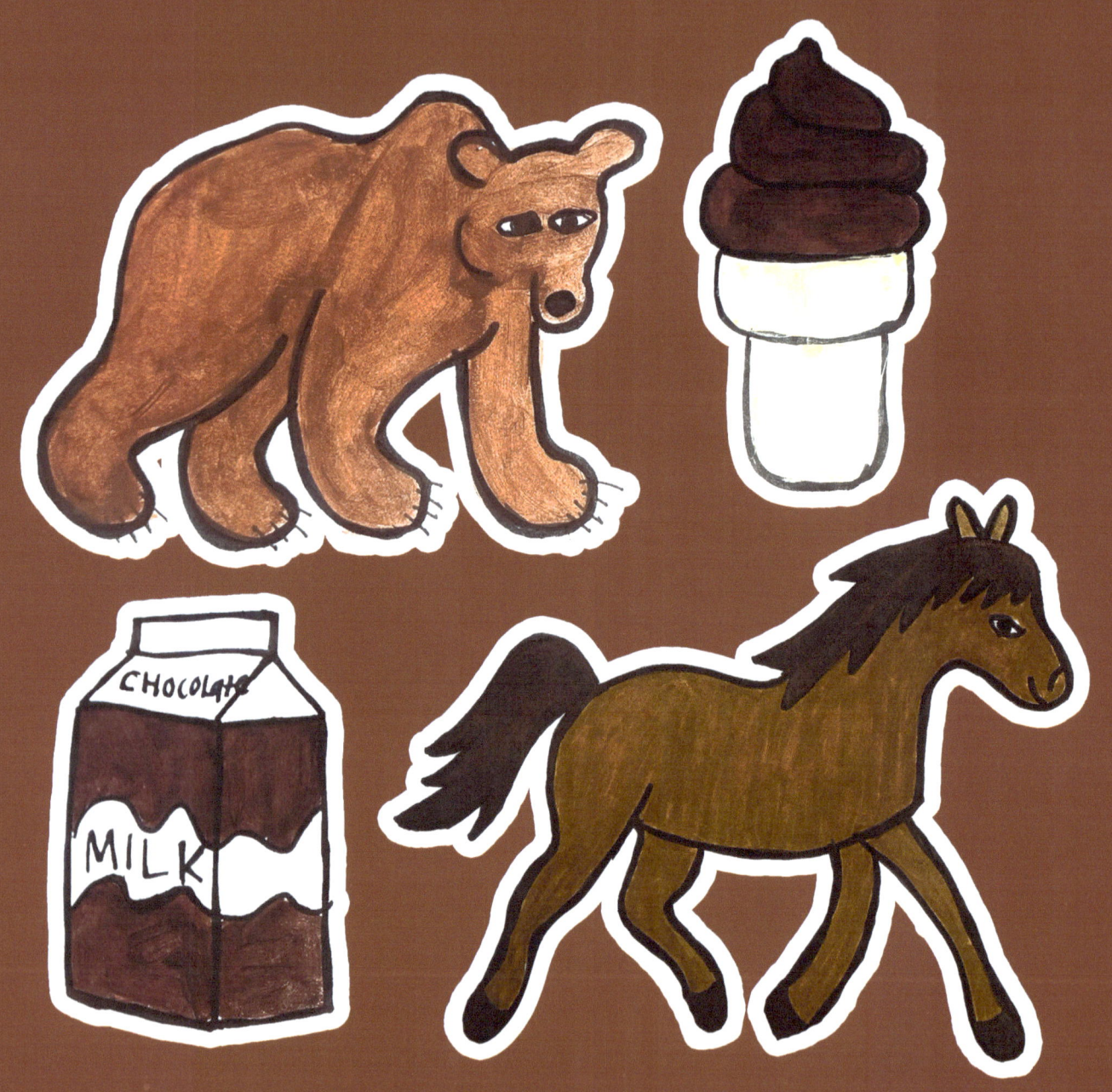

What is something that you know that's BROWN in color?

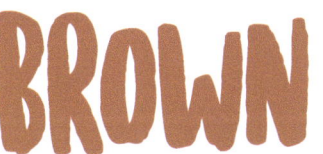

BROWN

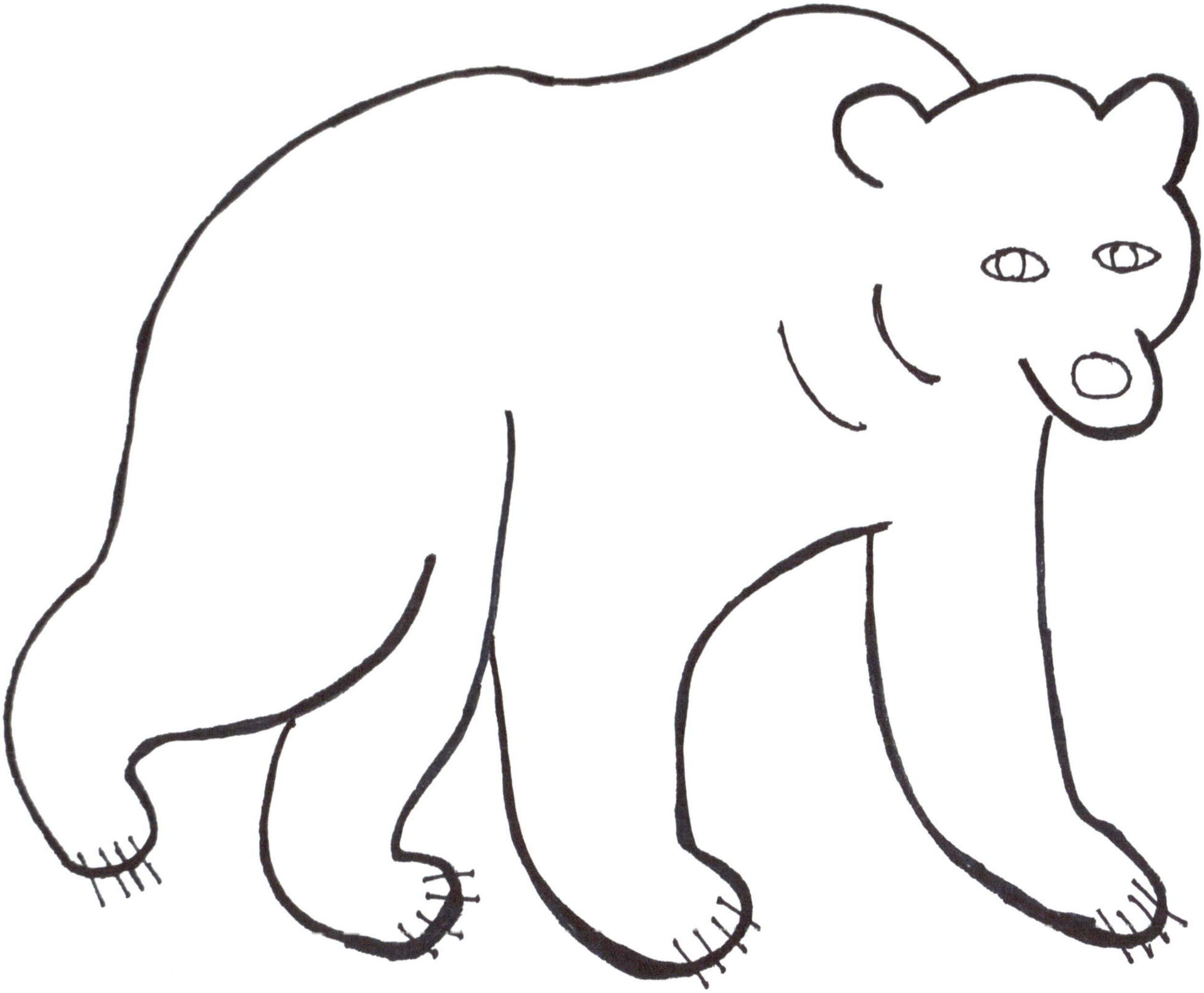

Color the BEAR the color BROWN.

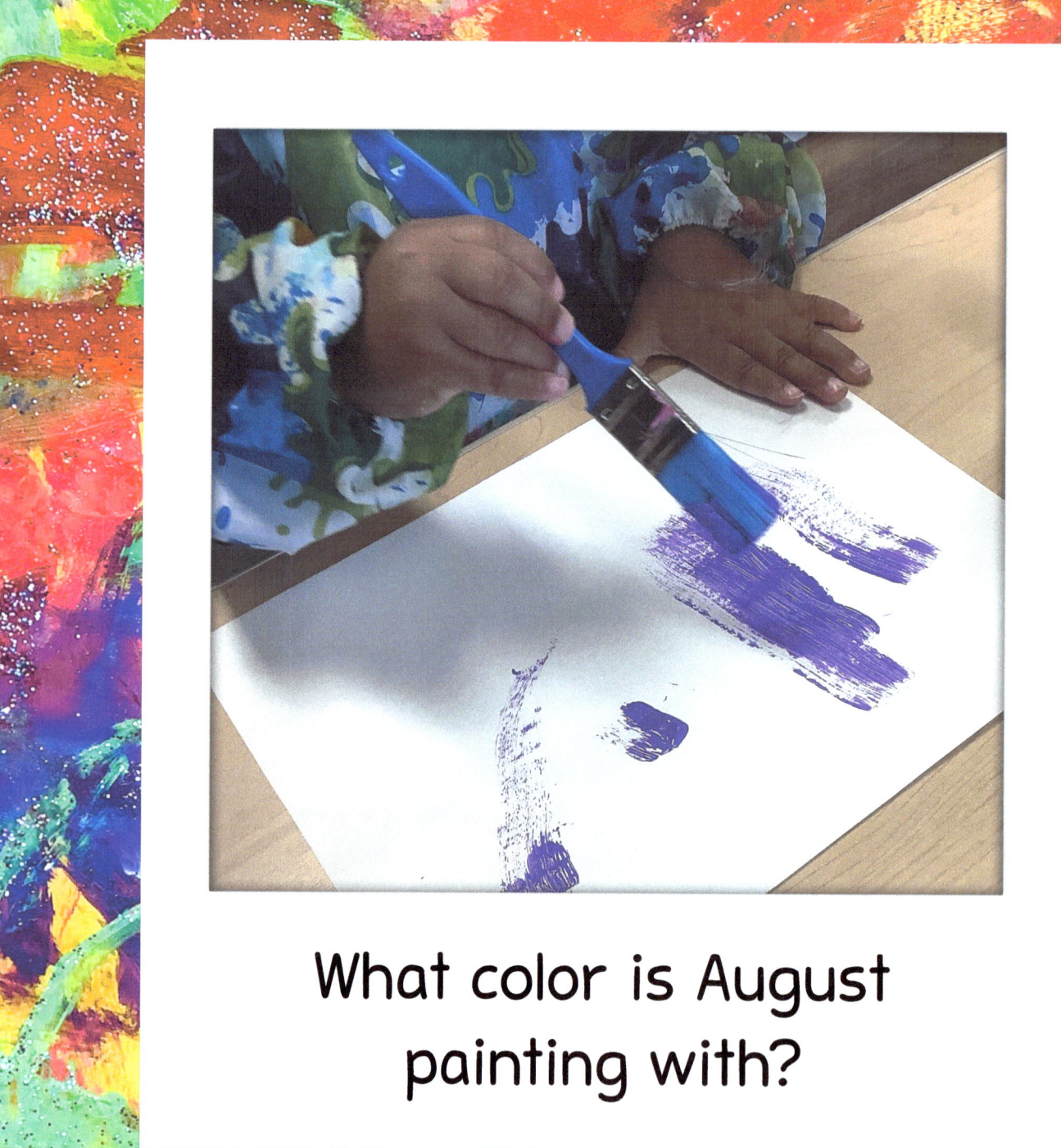

What color is August painting with?

PURPLE

August is painting
the color PURPLE.

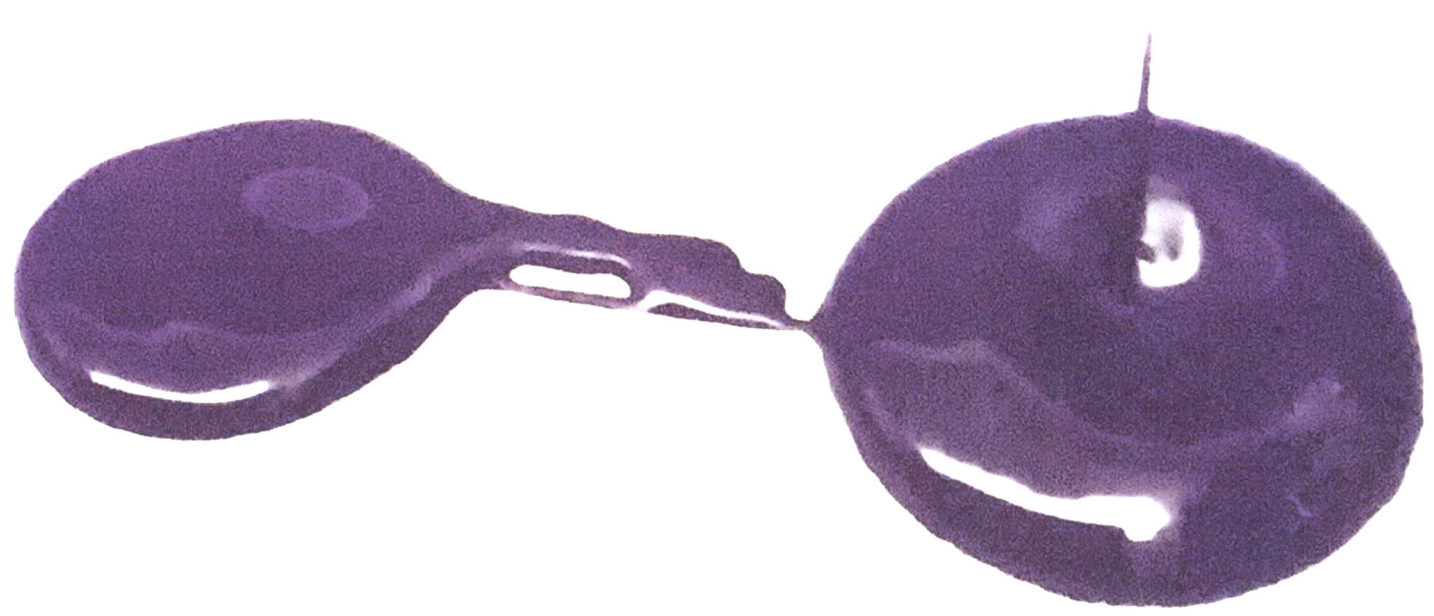

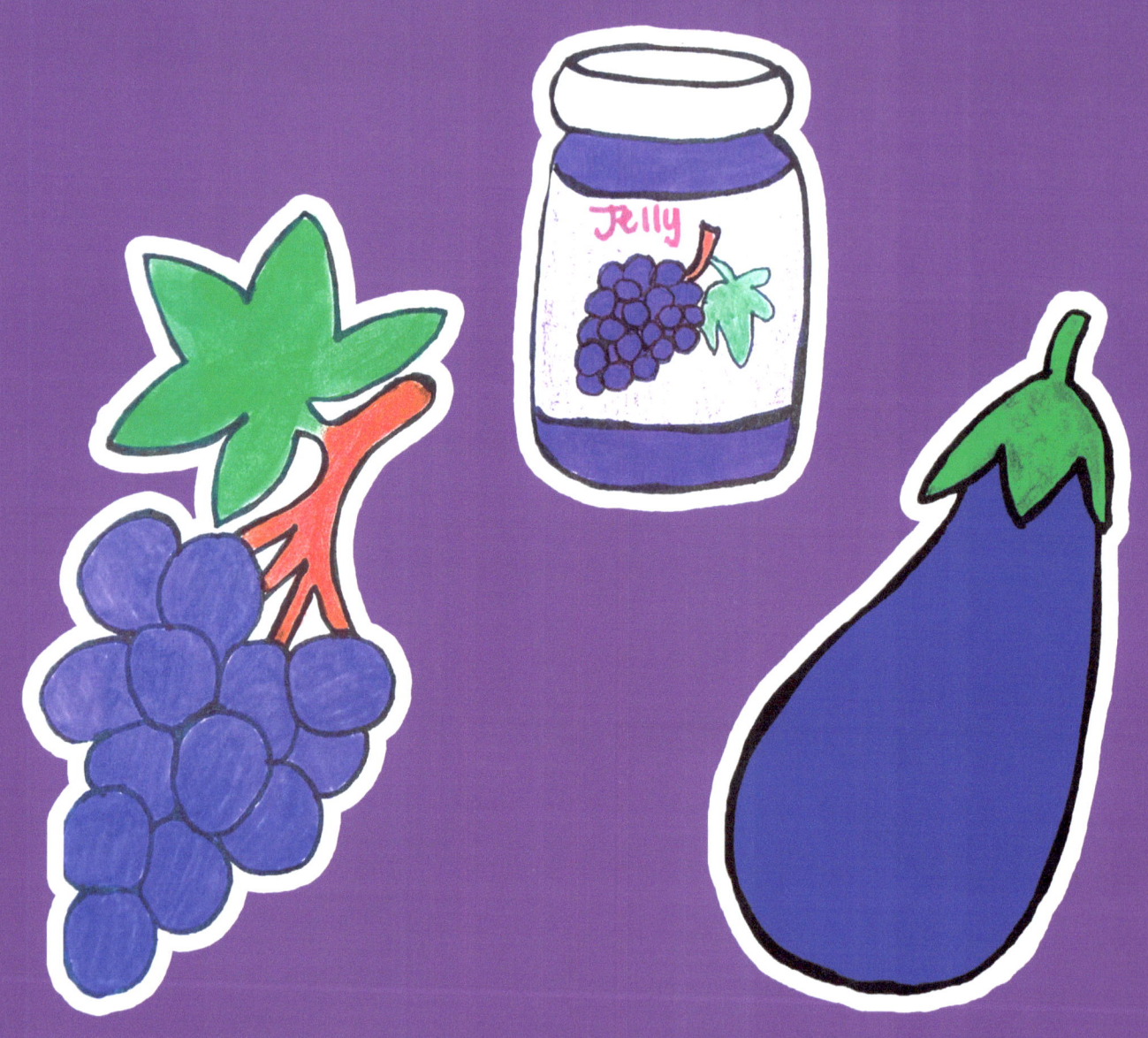

What is something that you know that's PURPLE in color?

PURPLE

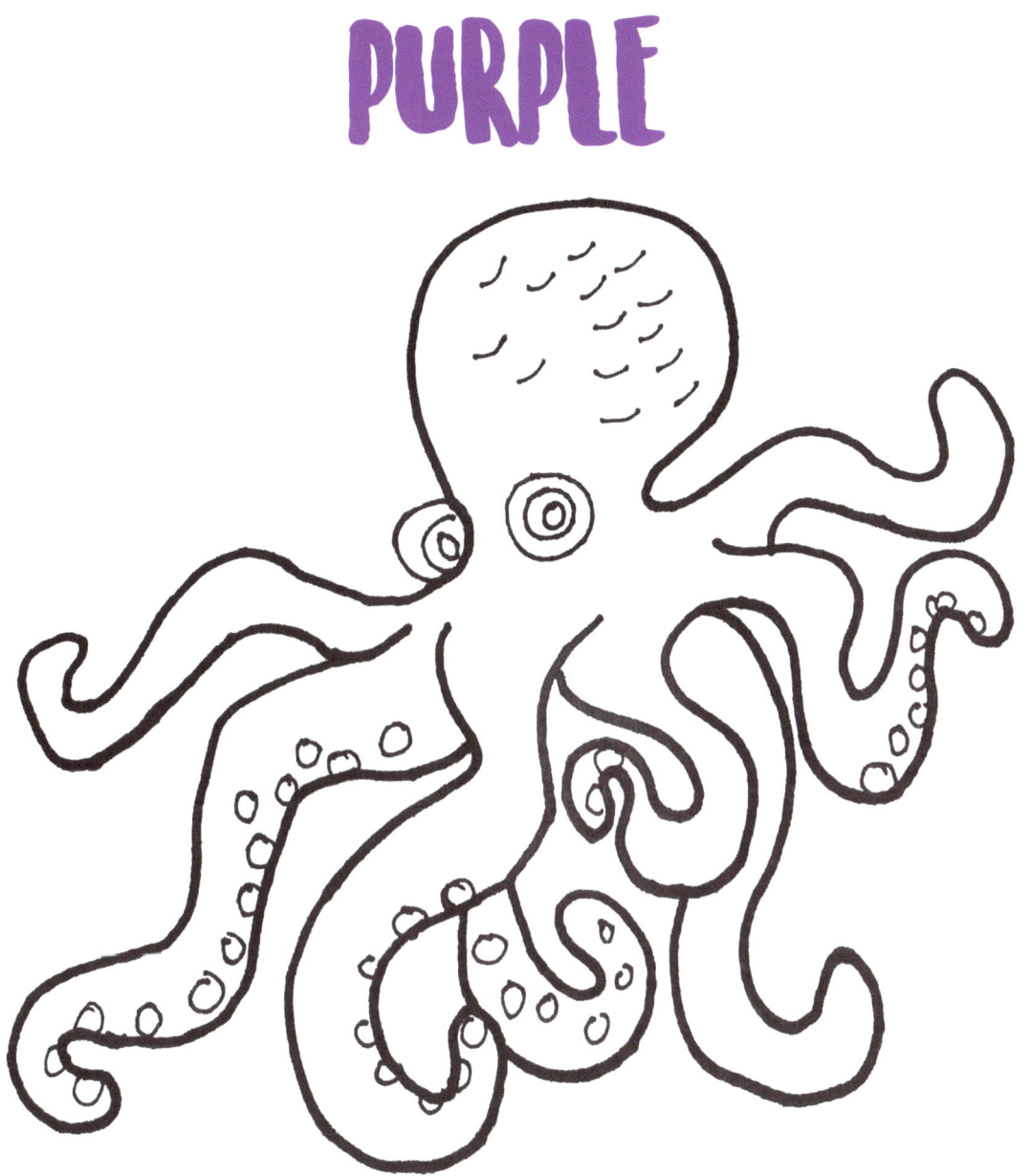

Color the OCTOPUS the color PURPLE.

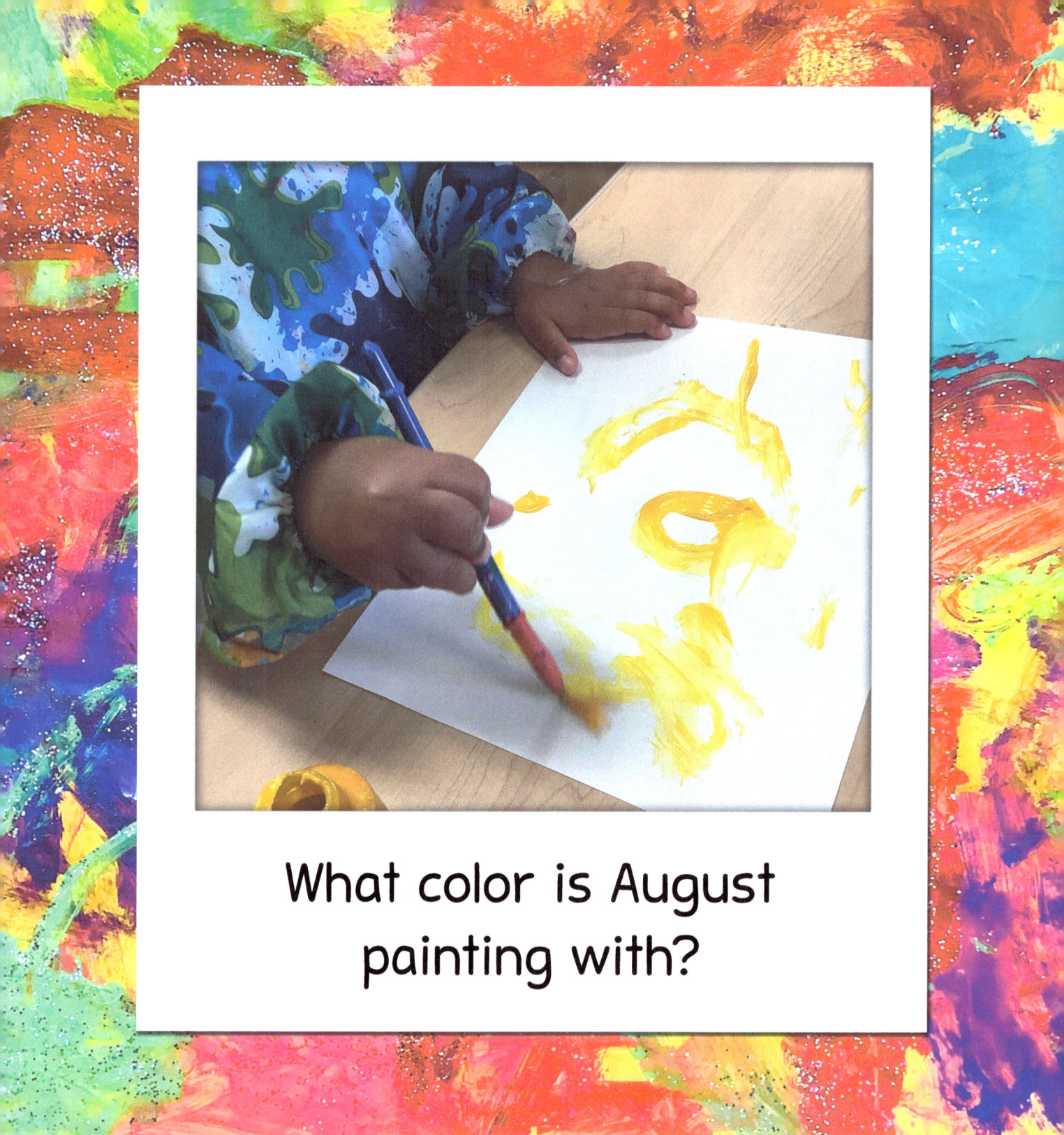

What color is August painting with?

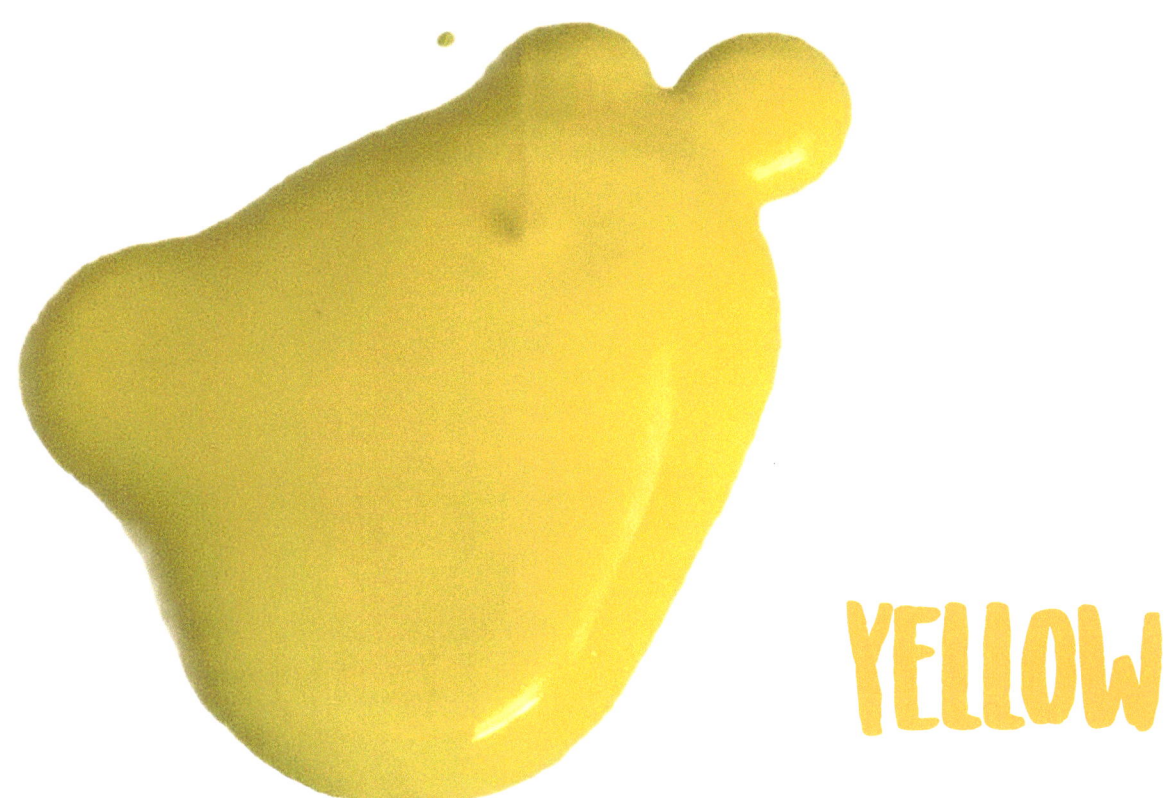

YELLOW

August is
painting with the
color YELLOW.

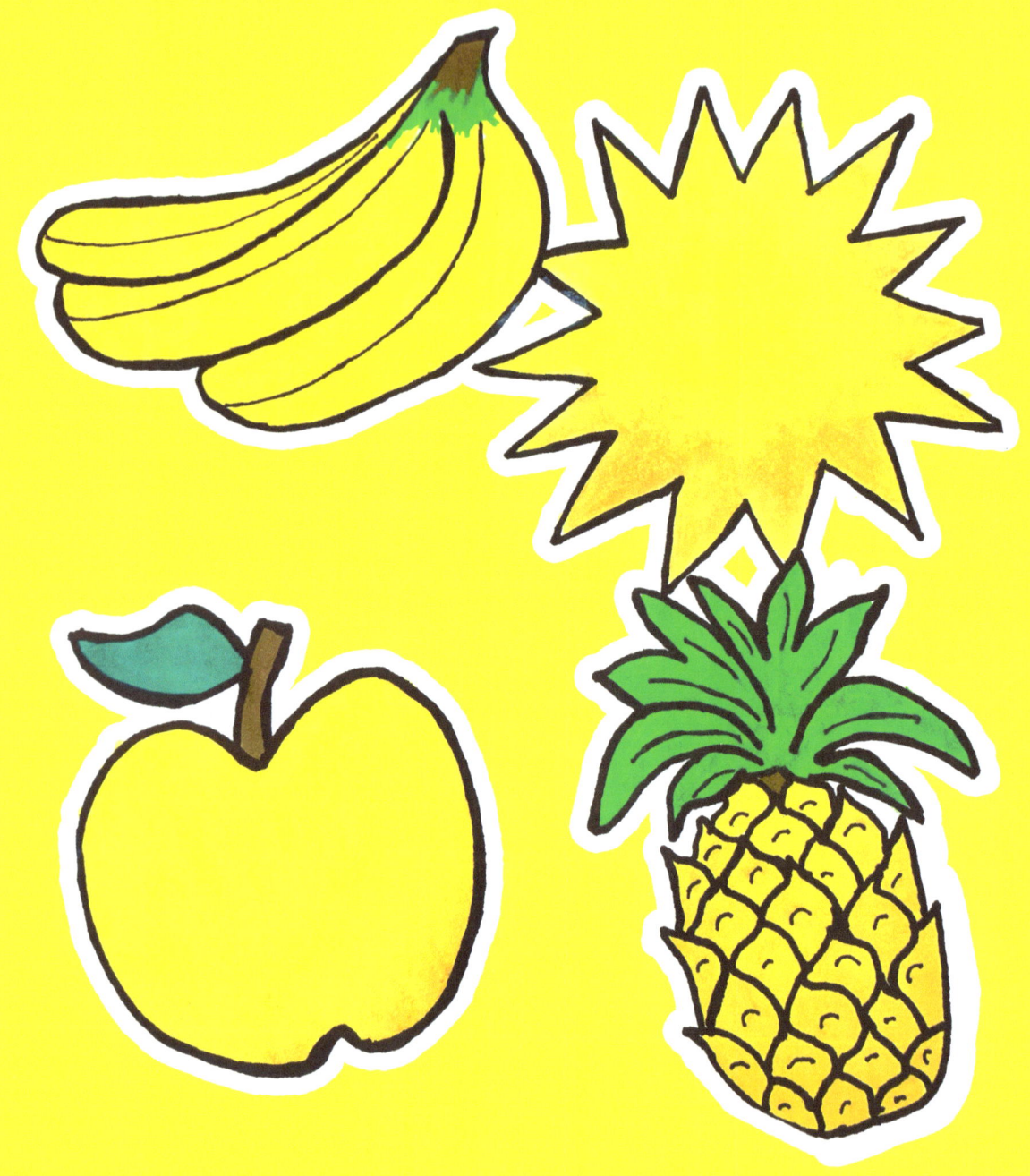

What is something that you know that's YELLOW in color?

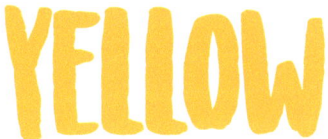

YELLOW

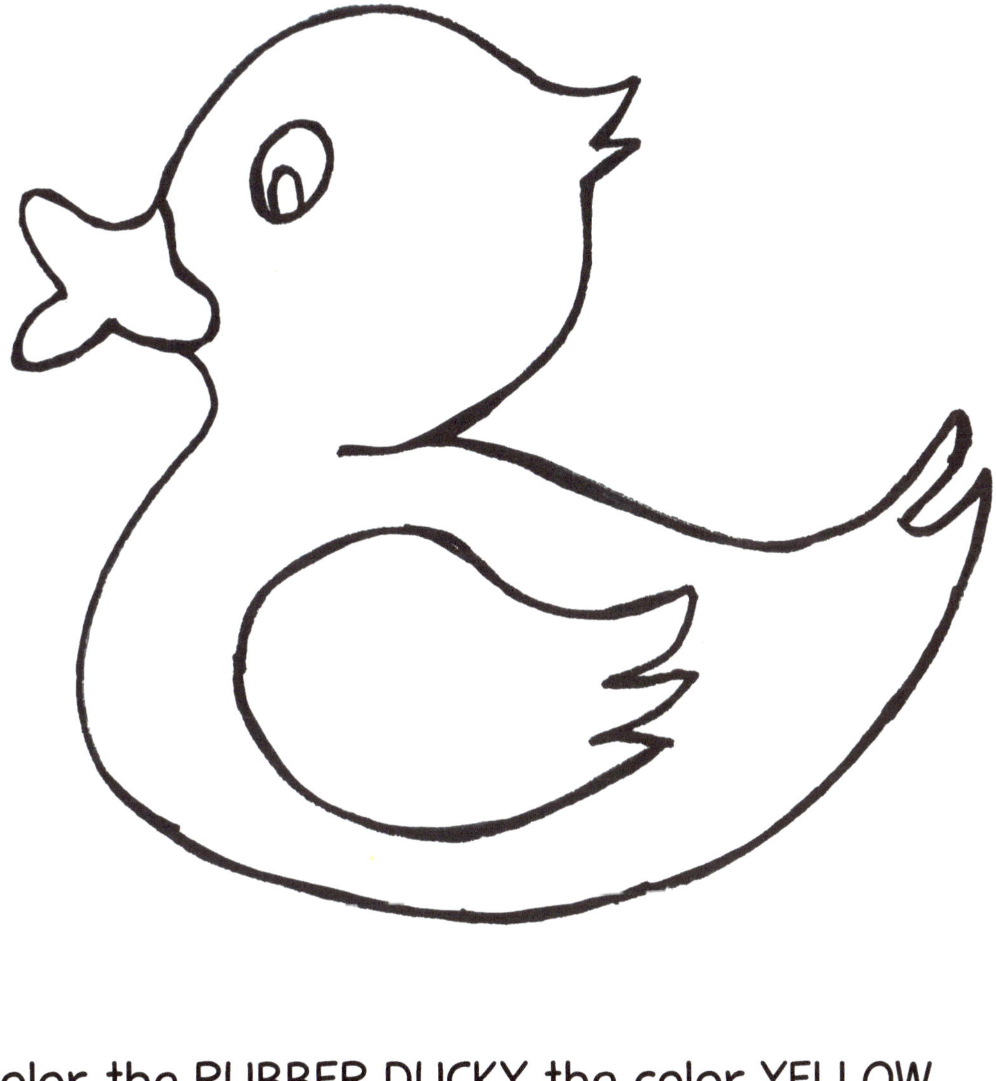

Color the RUBBER DUCKY the color YELLOW.

WHAT COLORS DO YOU SEE?

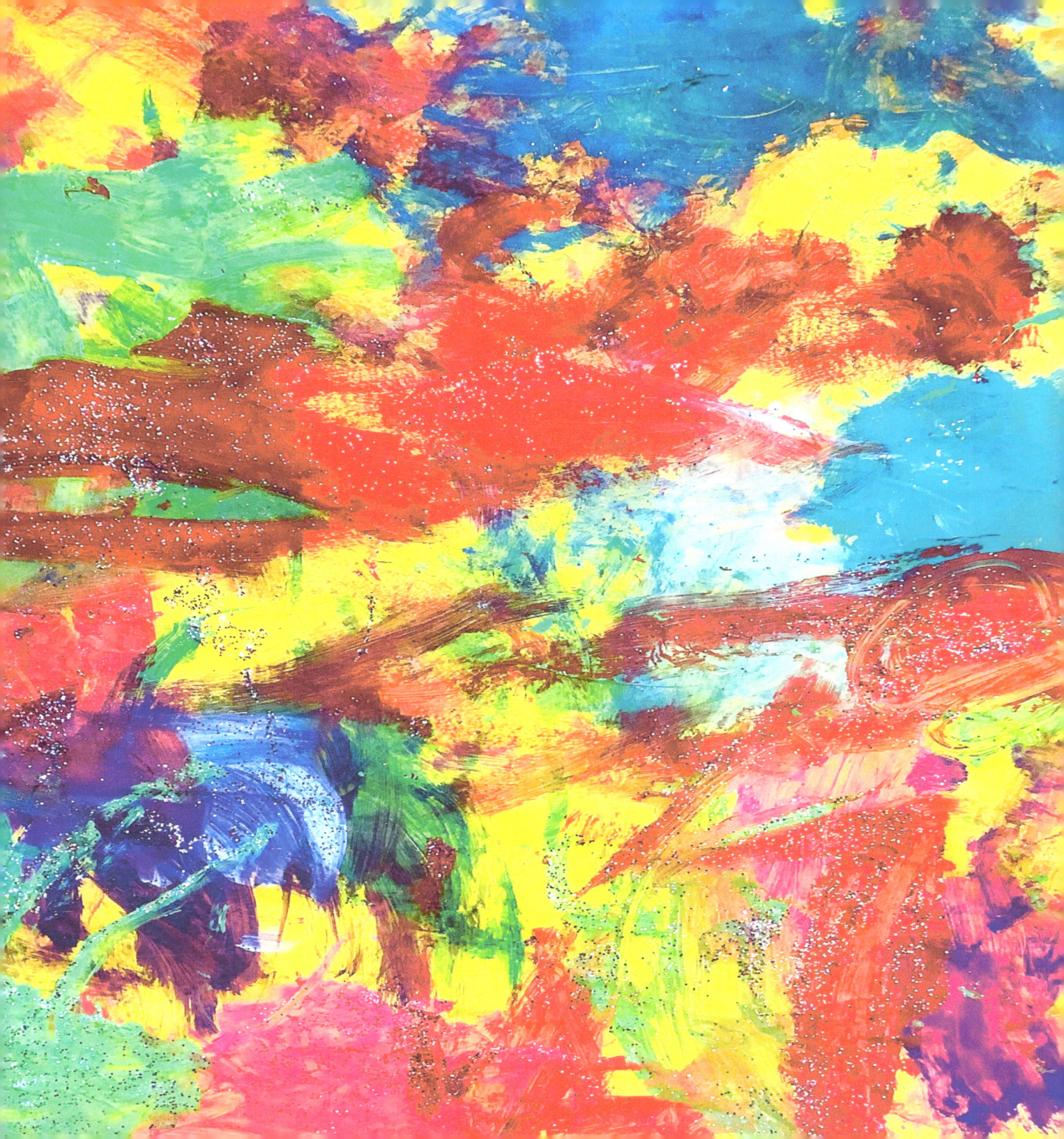

www.ingramcontent.com/pod-product-compliance
Lightning Source LLC
Chambersburg PA
CBHW041514280526
45792CB00004B/1248